THE WORSHIP MATRIX

THE WORSHIP MATRIX

Worship Planning as Journey and Exploration

by

Terry W. York and C. David Bolin

This book is a companion to www.WorshipMatrix.com

CELEBRATING Grace

WORSHIP & CHURCH
MUSIC RESOURCES

THE WORSHIP MATRIX
WORSHIP PLANNING AS JOURNEY AND EXPLORATION

ISBN 978-1-936151-14-1

10 11 12 13 14 15 16 17 18 19 20 – 10 9 8 7 6 5 4 3 2 1

MANUFACTURED IN THE UNITED STATES OF AMERICA

To Carl Bolin and Kate York, a father and a mother who showed their sons the doorways to the *Worship Matrix*.

FOREWORD

Terry York and David Bolin provide insight into the journey of discovery known as worship planning. The authors go beyond strategies to assemble an order of worship to a practical and meaningful place helping ministers approach worship planning with thoughtful research, community awareness, in-depth resourcing, and corporate engagement. Through *The Worship Matrix*, church leaders are taken to the creation point of corporate worship. It is not a cookie-cutter approach. *The Worship Matrix* philosophy allows for individual creativity, artistic expression, and meaningful exploration.

The most difficult parts of worship planning are not filling in the blanks of a set service, creating a worship map, or contacting people participating in a service. While these are important, they are matters of efficiency rather than fresh creativity. Time spent in prayer, research, and collaboration form the basis of the most time consuming, yet meaningful aspects of developing services of worship. York and Bolin focus on the "why" and "what" questions of this process. From philosophy to practical matters of worship space, they enable the reader to discover the level of personal contribution needed to plan worship.

While this book is a companion to the online *Worship Matrix* (www.WorshipMatrix.com), it is not an instructional manual. The online *Worship Matrix* does provide efficient planning tools, but goes beyond utilitarian functions. *Worship Matrix* serves as a guide for worship planners to find areas that will help worshipers encounter God. It enables planners to join with the people of our scriptural heritage such as Moses and Paul to great Christian leaders such as Luther and Wesley. Worship planners are encouraged to explore, collaborate, and enter worship planning through the portals of scripture, readings, hymns, themes, the Christian Year, resources available in the church's music library, and resources available in the Celebrating Grace family of products. York and Bolin provide the philosophical foundation of meaningful worship planning in this book. Furthermore, they give the reader a practical expression of using this philosophy through the online *Worship Matrix*.

John E. Simons
Coordinating Editor
Celebrating Grace Hymnal

TABLE OF CONTENTS

PROLOGUE

Intuitively, Christian worship seems a simple thing. But, the counter-intuitive fact is that Christian worship is a complex web of connections and entry points...a matrix.

God is not in a box, nor is God trapped under our steeples. There is no formula or ritual that will conjure God. Therefore, we should not seek only one door that will allow us to enter into worship. Further, even though people are sitting next to each other on a pew or in a row of chairs, even though they may be standing shoulder to shoulder, or bowing on neighboring kneelers, they may not actually engage in worship at the same time. In fact, we who plan and lead worship must make room for and honor the would-be-worshiper whose involvement on a particular Sunday will go no deeper than having their body at the right place at the right time. There is, indeed, something to be said for that bit of devotion.

No matter how much the worshipers may have in common, they come to the hour of worship from differing places of blessing and burden. Each of their entry points is present and valid. The worshiper does not invent them. The worship planner, under the guidance of the Holy Spirit, offers these points as invitations to enter; not to enter the presence of God, but to enter into worship. We are always in the presence of God. We are not always worshiping. One enters the corporate experience from their individual experience. At some point in the hour, all individual worshipers will sense the community of the worship matrix. This gathering of people and convergence of life experiences is Christian, it is Holy Spirit led, and it is in keeping with the priesthood of the believer and the proper path of the seeker. Whether those gathered proceed in the context of strict liturgy or "free-church" spontaneity, the concept of entering the matrix of Christian worship holds true.

What will not hold up in this model, or, for that matter, in any authentic Christian worship setting, is the idea of lock-step movement of all present from the outer courts to the holy of holies. But that should not surprise us. That is an Old Testament paradigm that, like all else, has been transformed by the birth, life, death, and resurrection of Jesus. The veil was "rent in twain,"(Mark 15:38) worship no longer has a group waiting in line at the one and only open door, and it must be noted, "the Lord is with you" whether you consider yourself to be in the outer courts or in the holy of holies.

In *The Worship Matrix*, the real life of this world's Monday through Saturday connects with the real life of worship in the context of eternity. The reality of individual experience connects with the reality of life in community. For the worshiper, their citizenship in the Kingdom of this world is in dynamic tension with their citizenship in the Kingdom of Heaven. Loyalties can be in conflict here. Further, their role as an individual worshiper is in dynamic tension with their role as a member of a worshiping community. Preferences and tendencies can be in conflict here. The worshiper may not be able to articulate these tensions, may not be conscious of their influence, but the worship planner must be aware. In this understanding of worship planning and worship participation, we no longer have to pretend that all tastes, preferences, and moods are being, or even can be, satisfied at the same time. Worship planning and worship leadership becomes a matter of inviting rather than ushering, of guiding a tour rather than calling cadence.

Community is an intertwining of paths. It is being up for the one who is down at the moment. Community's relationship to the individual is one of enhancing, encouraging, absorbing, healing, identifying, honoring, and commissioning. Community is giving and taking, individually, but individually in the same matrix and for the good of the whole. When choices about the inclusion of particular worship elements and the sequencing of those elements are made with the understanding that worship is a matrix, there is no "winning" preference or "losing" preference. All preferences, "waiting" to be chosen, exist in the matrix as contributions to the community's repertory.

It would seem one could argue, therefore, that the concept of worship being a matrix means that no worship planning is necessary. Just throw together some Jesus stuff and watch the Holy Spirit go to work as each person present steps up to this Sunday's buffet at the point of their preference or need. Of course, corporate worship is more than a collection of elements, just as the church is more than a gathering of individuals under the same steeple at the same hour.

Humans need structure in all aspects of life. No matter how independent from community one may seem, that person will establish or fashion their own routine. Structure is needed for comfort, for getting one's bearings, and as a foundation for progress. Christians have a divine call to community and to worship. Our contention, shared with many, is that the Holy Spirit's work, in any given worship experience, *begins* with worship planning; this includes pondering worship's structure. Worship planning is, under the guidance of the Holy Spirit, giving human structure to divine offering and invitation. Worship leadership is pointing to the path and giving aid to those who choose to journey there, no matter their starting point. The matrix that is worship is explored brand new each week, even in well-established liturgical settings and well-worn free-church routines. Indeed, the worship matrix is constructed brand new each week for each congregation at the junction of home and journey.

A new sense of community and "oneness" in Christ is experienced as each congregation realizes that their worship is part of a larger matrix environment with all Christian worship that has ever taken place and that ever will take place on earth and in heaven. The congregation can become aware of and increasing open to this relationship as they encounter over time, songs, litanies, and other worship expressions within their doctrinal boundaries, yet from other Christian traditions. Like individual persons becoming community under a particular steeple, differing Christian traditions and denominations find community in the common call to worship and allegiance to Jesus as Lord. All worship takes place in the context of the eternal now: God's matrix of time and eternity.

Perhaps the spiritual exercise of walking a "labyrinth" comes to mind as you consider the concept of worship being a "matrix" we enter since both are meant to be paths toward deeper spiritual focus and awareness. While we hold that worship is a journey and that worship should be characterized by an awe-inspiring sense of mystery, *Worship Matrix* is not presented in any sense of the mystical beyond the Holy Spirit's work of inviting and enabling believers to gather for the purpose of corporate worship. We offer this little book in the hope that it will ease some of the frustration of worship planning. Perhaps it will call some worship leaders to more thoughtful worship planning. We hope it might ease some of the tensions between those of differing worship styles, musical experiences, and loud/quiet tendencies. Perhaps this concept of entering the existing matrix at different points will ease the concern of the worship leader that there are some in the congregation who appear not to be participating.

Does this not allow for some to sit while others are standing? Does this not explain why some eyes are closed while others are open, why some are singing or reciting while others are silent? Is it not wonderful that we do not have to be judgmental or critical, and that we need not "evaluate" worship "effectiveness"? We no longer need to try to "outsmart" or "outmaneuver" the "non-worshiper." The concept of *Worship Matrix* assumes that the corporate experience will include a variety of expressions and responses, the very thing that happens anyway. This is not an excuse, it is an explanation. *Worship Matrix* is not a license for laziness in worship planning. It is not a computer program doing the work of the intertwined Holy and human spirits. *Worship Matrix* is an invitation to worship planning and the work of the Holy Spirit that begins there.

David Bolin
Terry W. York
Waco, TX

CHAPTER ONE

A Place for Guided and Unguided Discovery

Every congregation has work to do in finding the outward expressions that convey its inner life.

Located near busy central London, the Tate Britain is a treasure house of traditional and contemporary British art. This immense gallery holds close to 65,000 paintings, prints, photos, and sculptures in more than forty rooms. Some years ago, in an initiative to help visitors navigate the mammoth collection, a survey was conducted. Any visitor who appeared disoriented was approached by a researcher and asked if he was lost. In each case, a similar answer was given "Oh no, not at all." After declining this offer of assistance, however, the guests continued on their way still looking confused. The puzzled researchers surmised that no one really gets lost in an art exhibit because no one is trying to get anywhere. People do not go to a gallery to reach a particular destination but to enjoy the surroundings.

Galleries are intended as places in which to get lost. They yield their treasures as surprises, and the greatest of them draw repeat visitors by providing unexpected turns so that no one can discover all there is to find. There are, granted, advantages to the services of a guide. A guide tells the stories behind what you are seeing, takes you down paths you might not have taken, and points out the significance of things you could have ignored. Guides are certainly useful, but nevertheless, to experience a gallery, you must get lost in it for only then can you develop your own appreciation. And in your lost wanderings, you will come to appreciate the journeys of those who walked before you and with you through the matrix of the gallery.

In a sense, the entire universe can be thought of as a gallery ready for exploration in both guided and unguided ways. During the early years, our guides are both parents and teachers. They point to the heavens and show us the stars; they train our feet to kick the water until we can swim. Our guides teach us geography, geology, biology, paleontology, and a host of other "ologies" as we gain a sense of how vast is the universe and how small our place in it. But no amount of guided learning is a substitute for learning on our own — finding fingers and toes, hearing the ocean's roar, drinking in the fragrance of a plumeria blossom, or tasting a fat, luscious strawberry. Discovering by ourselves is how we discover ourselves.

The worship service, too, is a place for guided and unguided discovery. Unlike the gallery, however, where one is free to spend whatever length of time one desires before a work of art, the songs, readings, sermons, and ordinances present themselves in a sequence. And unlike the gallery holding relics of a bygone era, the worship service is a living thing inspiring new songs, art, and other expressions. The leader guides the congregation through the corridors of the prescribed liturgy, one drawn from the lectionary, of her own design, or that she, the pastor, and other service leaders plan together. Whatever the method, there is a starting point that moves to other points and on to a conclusion in orderly fashion. Some worship services are strongly didactic with an emphasis on a "teaching ministry." Other services are more free-flowing with an emphasis on "spontaneity." The common expectation, however, is that the members will start together, experience each service element together, and end together (right on the hour for some).

Led by professional worship leaders through the worship sequence, it is entirely possible for a congregation to say and sing the right words and never actually worship. The members may even surrender the saying and the singing to the worship leader. The outcome is a predictable service with the personality of the leader filling every nook and waiting at every turn. In time, the worship leader may come to think of the congregation as the instrument through which he worships and forget that the *leitourgia*, liturgy, is "the work of the people." That it truly is, but in what sense? Can the congregation as a whole actually plan a service and carry it out? If it could, would doing so even be advisable? The answer is a resounding "yes." It cannot be otherwise, for unless the people do their work, no worship takes place. This is why. Against the outward expressions of public worship, an unseen service is occurring within each worshipper who is the "temple of the Holy Spirit." The public expressions play out in time and sequence, but the inner experiences are timeless, transcendent, intersecting and diverging from the group expression (and Heaven itself) in ways unique to the individual. What is experienced outwardly in time and sequence is the prompting, the call to the inner reality. It is the word being sowed by the sower that becomes the living Word when received by the heart (Luke 8:4-8). How, when, and where the Word is received varies from person to person. In other words, the sequence in which the worshiper responds is different from the prompting of the outward expression.

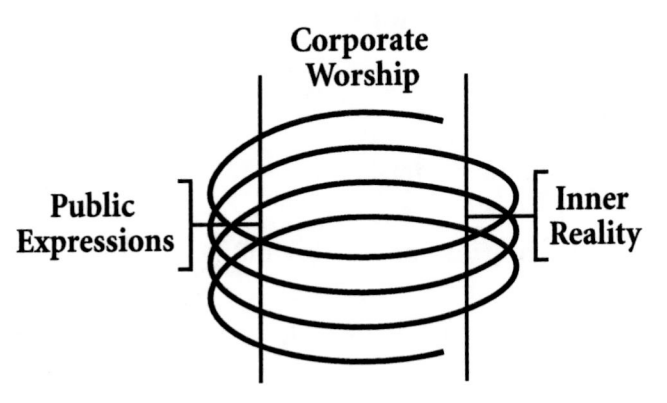

Here then is the premise of this book, and one which will be considered in the pages that follow. A worship service is a matrix through which each worshiper finds his or her own path. This is the way it has always been; the concept is not new, but it may be new to you to consider the matrix in worship design.

Let us suppose the service order lists the first activity as a "call to worship." We could assume then this is where worship will begin.

But will it really? See the middle-aged woman over there on the bench? She's agonizing over a disagreement she had with another worker in the hall. And look at that cute little boy near the front delighting in his first trip to a "big church." Oh, and there in that doorway stands a stranger, eyes quickly darting about looking for a familiar someone with whom to sit. Against all the inner cerebrations, the call to celebration sounds, but it may not be answered until later in the service as each individual responds to activities not designated as "the call." It is also true that as the initial call sounds, some people may already be worshipping, confessing sin, reflecting on scripture, "or making melody in their hearts to the Lord."

The psalmist said "He put a new song in my mouth, a hymn of praise to our God. Many will see and fear and put their trust in the LORD" (Psalm 40:3). The outward expression seen and heard is praise, but note that the inward response, unseen and unheard, is fear and trust.

The public expression could occur in this sequence:

praise - thanksgiving - confession - hearing - commitment

While the inner response might be:

confession - hearing - praise - commitment – thanksgiving

A call to worship is a call to walk the worship matrix wherever the path begins and however it unfolds. The leader who prays all the prayers, and demands the congregation hang on every word he has to say interrupts the Spirit wooing each person to follow. You have heard the exhortations to "just put all cares and thoughts aside and join me as we worship the Lord" meaning "stop thinking for yourself and do what I do or let me do it for you." As at the Tate Britain, this kind of guidance may not be something the worshipers want or will accept.

Let us consider how to stimulate one another to love and good deeds, not forsaking our own assembling together... (Hebrews 10:24-25)

The worship matrix cannot be seen, but the worship space can. As worship leaders work to make the visible things right, they may forget that we worship not in a holy place "made with hands" (1 Peter 3:24). In each worshiper's holy place speak the scripture writer, the hymn writer, and the composer. Joining their voices are voices remembered from other times and places. The voices speak to individual concerns, fears, hopes, and longings. Knowledge is gained, understandings reached, commitments made which then give impetus to singing a song, passing the peace, saying a prayer, or reading the scripture. By these outward manifestations springing from the inner dialogue, worshipers are encouraged along their individual paths in the worship matrix.

What then is the role of the worship planner? Returning to the art gallery analogy, she is best considered as curator. The curator does not produce the art on display but organizes it into an exhibit that visitors to the gallery can explore at the pace and path of their choosing. The curator determines a starting point–the art of a particular civilization–the ancient Mayans, let us say. She then works outward in all directions from that point–painting, clothing, sculpture, tools–linking the artifacts to world history and anthropology. She knows that though the visitor will not begin at the same place as she, her starting place can be found because the connections exist. In like manner, the worship planner begins with a scripture verse, a song text, a sermon idea and works out in all directions. He links the text with other verses, songs, testimonies, and the life of the community into an exhibit of God's presence and grace which is broad and diverse enough to be meaningful to everyone. How this process works will be explored in depth throughout the book, but here is a brief description illustrated by text of the popular worship song "Here I Am to Worship."

"Light of the world
You stepped down into darkness"

Think of all the directions this short phrase could go!

It links us to creation.

Then God said, "Let there be light"; and there was light. God saw that the light was good; and God separated the light from the darkness. God called the light day, and the darkness He called night. (Genesis 1:3-5)

It is the fulfillment of prophecy.

The people who walk in darkness will see a great light; Those who live in a dark land, The light will shine on them.
(Isaiah 9:2)

It tells who Jesus is.

In Him was life, and the life was the Light of men. The Light shines in the darkness, and the darkness did not comprehend it.
(John 1:4-5)

It lays claim to Christ's lordship over every nation and ruler.

See, darkness covers the earth and thick darkness is over the peoples, but the LORD rises upon you and his glory appears over you. Nations will come to your light, and kings to the brightness of your dawn.
(Isaiah 60:2-3)

It calls us to discipleship.

...for you were formerly darkness, but now you are Light in the Lord; walk as children of Light. (Ephesians 5:8)

It calls us to fellowship with one another.

This is the message we have heard from Him and announce to you, that God is Light, and in Him there is no darkness at all. If we say that we have fellowship with Him and yet walk in the darkness, we lie and do not practice the truth; but if we walk in the Light as He Himself is in the Light, we have fellowship with one another, and the blood of Jesus His Son cleanses us from all sin. (1 John 1:5-7)

It promises deliverance.

Light arises in the darkness for the upright; He is gracious and compassionate and righteous.
(Psalm 112:4)

It commissions us as witnesses.

But you are a chosen race, a royal priesthood, a HOLY NATION, a people for God's own possession, that you may proclaim the excellencies of Him who has called you out of darkness into His marvelous light. (1 Peter 2:9)

As you've read these verses, you have undoubtedly thought of other scriptures which link to these lyrics. All this comes from just the first two lines of the song! The power of a text is in its capacity to connect with scripture and other songs providing a wealth of places to visit in the worship matrix. But it does not end there. Each associated scripture connects with still other songs and other scripture texts with additional truth to explore. A mistake is made when songs are chosen primarily for their emotional content–because they are "high-energy" or "worshipful". Unite a strong text to strong emotional content, though, and the song will speak throughout the service and lead to other places in the worship matrix.

"In my Father's house are many rooms." (John 14:2)

Moving through the matrix is not unlike the way people study the Bible. If every verse were to be thought of as a unique room, then at this very moment, most, if all not all the rooms, are being visited by someone somewhere in the world. There are the well-read verses, or rooms, peopled by many readers and other more obscure verses visited by but a few. All the rooms, however, are inhabited by someone and God is speaking in them all. If we were to diagram this dynamic, our drawing would resemble a giant matrix, teeming with energy with movement from room to room. And if we, ourselves, were to move through the rooms, what was heard in one would send us to the next, and what was heard in the next would send us to another, and so on, and so on. We, also, would keep returning to rooms already visited to reconsider what God is saying in the context of what we heard in other places. So, a person may begin reading the gospels, reference the Pauline epistles and be directed to the Old Testament prophets. To study the scripture is to move from century to century, place to place, and people to people. One can almost hear the various writers discussing an issue. There are many factors that determine what room a reader chooses to visit–a story's appeal, a current crisis, what is already known and what is not. The point is that no two readers are the same, and even when several inhabit the same room, what each hears God saying will in some degree be different.

The Bolins are shopping for a new home. After years of taking care of a large yard, we are looking for something smaller with a yard someone else can mow. When we visit an open house, we take off to different corners, at some point cross each other's path and end up where the other started–same house, same family, different routes. As we cross, something may be said like "nice master" or "small closets" letting the other know what can be expected to be seen on the other side of the house. When we have a serious interest in a place, we will visit it several times taking different routes, experiencing the rooms in different sequences until we know the house well enough to make an offer. Of course, one cannot really know a house until it has been lived in for several years.

The worship service is a foreshadowing of Heaven where Christ said there are "many rooms." Little is known of how the early church conducted its worship, but in this verse of Paul's instruction to the church in Corinth the matrix is evident.

> When you come together, everyone has a hymn, or a word of instruction, a revelation, a tongue or an interpretation. All of these must be done for the strengthening of the church.
> (1 Corinthians 14:26)

The first Christ followers came from different corners bringing gifts by which all believers were nurtured and encouraged. A hymn, a word of instruction, a revelation–by these gifts the rooms in which they gathered were defined. Inwardly, however, each member visited in his own time what together all had established. The praise song, sung by all voices in the beginning, was echoed by a heart later in the service to something else the ears heard. Inner experience begets outward expression which begets inner experience. One gives birth to another.

The Quakers believed any outward expression in worship was to be preceded by the prompting of Christ in the heart of the believer who spoke. The congregation waited in silence until someone exercised the "vocal ministry" in response to Christ's moving. This is how all Quaker worship was conducted until the late nineteenth century when the vocal ministry diminished and the spiritual life of the congregations seemed depleted. At the same time, revivalism was sweeping America. Many Quakers attended the meetings, experienced conversion, and started their own "programmed" services. Today, in North America about two-thirds of Quaker services are considered programmed. The outward expression of the revivalism brought new vitality to Quaker worship. Outward expression begat inner experience which begat outward expression. One gave birth to the other.

"I would rather be a doorkeeper..." (Psalm 84:10 KJV)

The decor of our house reflects the many years we lived in Honolulu. It is Asian in design, filled with objects reminding us of people and places we love. We are not unique in surrounding ourselves with things that tell our story. Urban, transitional, or traditional–people select the style that makes them feel at home. Walk through the house, hear the stories, and you will learn who the family is who lives there. A worship service is also telling. Join the singing, the responsive readings, and the prayers; listen to the sermons and testimonies, and you will walk the matrix of the congregation's life, the holy place where the Lord resides.

Every congregation has work to do in finding the outward expressions that convey its inner life. The choices will be affected by theology, history, and tradition. They must also be true to the congregation's personality, diversity and the skills of its membership. In a church startup situation where there are no members, the demographic makeup of the community will become a primary consideration. A church plant in a town 90% Hispanic will naturally take that statistic into account, and when a community surrounding an established congregation changes, those changes may also affect service planning. This is all well and good, but congregations should not be quick in abandoning their uniqueness to redecorate the rooms for church prospects or to accommodate the style preferences of a new worship leader. Predictably, doing so will board up the familiar doors through which long-time members enter the worship matrix. The complaints heard about changes to the worship service may have nothing to do with musical style, or service length, or room comfort, or any of the things people actually say. What may being said is: "We can no longer find a way in. We keep marching around the walls of the city, but the walls won't come down!"

There is no point in ushering one group out of the worship matrix in order to invite another group inside, nor is there need. Remember, it is the different perspectives, the "everyone has a hymn, or a word of instruction, a revelation" that makes the rooms worth visiting. It is the many dimensions of the matrix that enable one to explore the height, the depth, and the breadth of Godliness.

The worship planner is the doorkeeper, opening room after room for people to enter. Like the gallery guide, he knows the congregation's story and understands the significance of rooms that might be ignored. He reminds the worshipers they are not the artists but God's workmanship, that He is remaking them, rearranging the rooms, and leading them on paths through the matrix they would not otherwise have followed. The planner keeps the paths clear for exploration through good worship design that minimizes the impediments that might hinder worshipers as they move from room to room. Through it all, the planner must be careful not to repeat the same tour spiel week after week, filling each room with himself and demanding everyone enter the matrix at the same spot, the same time, and in the same way. He knows that he is not the mediator between the worshipers and God, only the doorkeeper. He opens the doors, invites all to enter and points out all the directions they are free to go. In the following chapters, we will consider the different doorways to be opened.

There are no Sunday strolls through the worship matrix. One does not enter or leave without effort and confusion, but then that is what it means to be "lost in wonder, love, and praise." Being lost means that things will not come together in a neat, little package; it means that some parts of the service will not be fully understood. Every worshiper must ask, seek, and knock on the doors of the worship matrix before they open and fellowship with Christ is enjoyed; and fellowship with Him and the people with whom the rooms are shared is the goal.

CHAPTER TWO

Entering Through the Word

Many people will enter into worship through worship's words. They will listen for the poetry that lifts like earth-born mists of prayer to meet with Heaven-bound clouds of praise. They will listen for the engagement of real life prose with God's real words of forgiveness, hope, and promise. That's where many will stand and listen before they enter into worship.

Words are a big deal to God. God *spoke* creation into being. Then, when creation needed to be redeemed, "The Word became flesh and lived among us..." (John 1:14a). We who have been redeemed are admonished to "Let the word of Christ dwell in [us] richly..." (Colossians 3: 16a). Something seems to be going on here.

We certainly know the importance of words in worship. From language that includes rather than excludes, to ancient words that carry deep meaning and tradition, to words of hope, we come to worship listening for the voice of God in the words we read and hear. As we are invited to sing, read aloud, and pray, we find God's words coming from within us. We are worshipers and we are priests. Worship is made real, personal, and even internal as the words flow from us to God.

REVELATION AND MYSTERY: A DYNAMIC TENSION

Words anchor two ends of an important dynamic tension in Christian worship. At one level we might describe this tension as being between what is familiar to us and what is new to us. At a deeper level, this same dynamic tension can be characterized as being between what God has revealed about himself and the mystery that remains. Continuing along this line of thought, the words of our worship can expand our vision of the vastness of God or they can be used to reduce God to someone easily understood and who is in our employ. Pulling God down to our size and agenda is not worship. Yet, God with us (Immanuel) is the beginning of Christian worship. Words help us know and express the difference.

What we know about God is the result of God's self-revelation through one means or another. But we should not assume that what we know about God is all there is to know or that it is all we need to know as followers. The words of our worship can reduce our congregation's concept of God in this way, even though it is not our intention for that to happen.

Words that express God's self-revelation are important, but they must be matched with words that express the continuing mystery of God. We must know that God is bigger than us and our needs, even than our desires. It is important to us to be reminded each Sunday that God's wisdom and love and power are beyond our imaginations. Such awareness will be the work of words; carefully chosen, spoken, sung, prayed, and preached words.

THE WORD MADE FLESH

"In the beginning was the Word, and the Word was with God, and the Word was God." (John 1:1). The Word *is* Jesus and words of life come *from* Jesus. The function of "word" expands as God creates, communicates, and redeems. As we read and hear scripture (God's holy word) the Holy Spirit seems to whisper silent words of understanding, insight, and guidance into our hearts and lives. The more we listen, the more we learn to detect the Holy Spirit's whisper and understand the words.

At the risk of creating false intrigue or trying to appear unusually insightful, we share a passing thought: why "word?" What would it be like if the *Melody* had become flesh or the *Note*, the everlasting Perfect Pitch, dwelt among us? Why not let the *music* of Christ dwell in you richly? Words are not the only foundational element of human expression. Music is important to every culture. Notes are foundational.

What would be the implications if the *Number* became flesh and dwelt among us? We can imagine the eternal One, having numerical implications. The eternal One lives in the vast infinity. Zero would represent the absence of God. Math represents both revelation and mystery, as does music, as do words. Perhaps math is too much a matter of the mind and music too much a matter of the heart. Words function with specificity and image in both arenas.

Whatever the reason, in God's wisdom it was the Word that became flesh; the Word who is the truth in image and application. Words are at once specific and general, descriptive and suggestive. In the case of Jesus, the Word is at once divine and human. Words can give us instructions for microwaving a frozen meal, and they can suggest the beauty of a sunset on a yet-to-be-discovered planet. Jesus spoke words of instruction and parable. Jesus, fully human, said while dying, "I thirst." He wanted water. That same Jesus, fully God, earlier had said "Peace, Be Still" and an entire sea responded in submission. Words are powerful and revealing.

The right word at the right time can bring two people together. In contrast, the wrong word at the wrong time can keep two people apart for a lifetime; a simple, single word. A word can convey promise or despair. Words can inspire or crush, release or enslave. We are speaking, of course, of communication, precise or purposefully vague. Community, communication, culture: words are the basic currency of each of these human projects. Is it any wonder that words are a common entry point into worship? For some, words are simply a necessary entry point to be assumed, even taken for granted.

For others, words are things of art and beauty. They are something to be savored.

Words are entry points that swing open or slam shut (Matthew 7:7-8; Luke 13:24-25). The words we use in worship should be well-oiled hinges that swing doors open. Our words should be as inclusive, as welcoming, and as warm as the One we worship. Words matter, even if they are from a Christian worship vocabulary somewhat different from our particular tradition or are entirely new to the seeker us.

Shall we write, print, pray, sing, or speak flippant, throw-away words in our worship of *The* Word? The thought is at least embarrassing; it borders on repulsive. If we are going to engage in something that we hope will be received as worship, our words had better be authentic and honest. Each word should be seasoned with tears and truth that welcome yet humble the worshiper and honor the One being worshiped.

Indeed, words can flesh out the Christ and his teachings in the context of worship. There are some people who engage the spoken word more clearly or more quickly than they do the sung word. They are listening for the poetic moment or subtle insight or the well crafted phrase as an invitation to participate in worship at a deep level. The words of worship, throughout the hour should say "You are welcome here," even if they are new words to the novice worshiper. "Come in now, through this door. Your heart is summoned." Your name has been called, and it is a word or a grouping of words that has gotten your attention. Come, join those who enter through other doors, but gather in this same room, at this same time, for the same purpose: to worship.

THE POETRY OF WORSHIP

Poet, playwright, and pastor Ragan Courtney speaks of poetry in this way: "The language that we must speak must be reclaimed by those who long to be eloquent. It is our 'mother tongue' that has been spoken since the garden; it is the beautiful language of poetry. There is no other way by which we can talk of the lofty and holy things of God."[1]

Words stand at the far edge, at the final extent and reach of specification in human expression. But words are not stopped at the far boundary of specification. Words can take another step. The next step for words is poetry. Finally, even poetry reaches its far extent and human vocabulary moves to moans. The Holy Spirit has to take it alone from there, interpreting human groans.

> Likewise the Spirit helps us in our weakness; for we do not know how to pray as we ought, but that very Spirit intercedes with sighs too deep for words.
> (Romans 8: 26)

Like poetry, worship stands at the far edge and final extent of human expression. For worship, the far edge, the final extent is submission and commitment. But, like the poetry of language, the poetry of worship has a next step. The next step for worship is selfless availability when liturgical actions, motions, and ritual have played their part but have not given full expression to the depth and extent of our devotion Again, the Holy Spirit has to take it alone from there, this time interpreting human martyrdom. Poetry is a powerful art form. Worship is a powerful statement.

Worship exists on that border where the revelation of God blends into and gives way to the mystery of God. In similar fashion, one might define poetry as an artful crafting of words that has meaning at the surface and points to a deeper meaning still. This could easily be said of worship itself. It has meaning at the surface for all who are present, yet it points to something deeper.

---

[1] Ragan L. Courtney, Wesley L Forbis, and Terry W. York. *Three Voices: Poetry in Worship*, Nashville: Convention Press, 1994, dust cover.

But those surface points of entry into the deeper meaning of worship will not be the same for everyone. The worship planner must remember that. Even if all worshipers did engage in worship at the same time, poetry reminds us that we should not expect worshipers to move from Entrance to Dismissal in lockstep.

Poetry is not about controlling the reader. Worship is not about controlling the congregant. Ask a poet what she was trying to say in a particular poem and she will probably respond with the question, "What did it say to you?" If we should ask a worship planner/leader "What were you trying to say through today's worship?" The proper response, similar to that of the poet's, would be, "What did you say to God in worship, and what did you hear God saying to you?" This is difficult for even the most humble worship planner/leader. Are we not supposed to accomplish something in worship? How will we know if we did it right or could have done it better if there are not measurable goals or observable reactions?

Poetry does not function like pointed prose. Worship does not function like a sales meeting. The poet gives up a great deal of control over the hearer/reader. This is also the case in authentic worship: individual perceptions and perspectives of pace, direction, and response are left to the Holy Spirit. They are not manufactured and secured. The poet is trying to say something that is grander than words can express. The poet is pointing with heart, mind, and soul to the source and the object of their work. The worship planner/leader is pointing with heart, mind, and soul to the source and object of worship.

At their best, poetry and worship invite participation and engagement, even though there is an imposed sequence to the words that are read, spoken, sung and heard. Like writing poetry, planning and leading worship require faith; faith that the pointing and inviting is not only sufficient, but is, indeed, their only assignment. The poet and the worship planner/leader must have faith that their work will be completed in a spiritual dimension beyond their control, even beyond their understanding. If faith is not required because the poet and the planner have written-in prescribed summations and conclusions, one must wonder if poetry has been sacrificed for mere rhyming, and worship has been sacrificed for mere manipulation. There is a reason the poet writes and a reason the minister plans. There is purpose and hope in both efforts. But the poet listens to the poem, even as he writes, and the minister listens to the developing worship, even as she plans.

Poetry requires something of the reader. The reader is very much a partner in this artistic, communicative enterprise. The frustrated reader of poetry might say in disgust, "Why doesn't the poet just say what they mean?" The answer, of course, is that poetry is about what you "mean," what the poem causes you to see and say from within. Like poetry, worship requires something of the worshiper. The worshiper is very much a partner in the spiritual enterprise. "Why don't the worship planners and leaders just say what they mean?" Often they do, perhaps most often. But, similar to the poet's answer, worship is a time for you to say what you mean and to join with the community in saying what, together, you mean. The poet and the worship planner/leader respect these vital partners and would not presume to script or control their partners' journey into the mystery. Real poets, worship planners, and worship leaders stand in awe of the spiritual aspects of their work and are humbled by it. They are surprised by the responses to and interpretations of their particular poetry. Neither good poetry nor good worship ties a bow of completion at the end. Rather, they send the participant out into the responsibility and mystery of application.

Imagery is important in poetry and in worship. The words must paint a picture. We would expect this to be said of the sermon, and, indeed, it will be in just a few paragraphs from now. But, all words in the context of worship must, and do, paint pictures, and we know that different people see different things in any work of art.

I have in my office a framed work of art by Betty Wood. I know nothing about the artist. I purchased the work, identified as the 48th of 125 copies, in an "antique" store in a small central Texas town. To the best of my limited analytical and descriptive abilities, the image is white lines (perhaps one continuous line) on a blue background. The lines curve and wander, creating two near-circles in the midst of in-tertwined and distorted ovals (sorry Betty). Framed, the piece is approximately 12" by 14". The artist has titled the work, "Mother and Child."

When I show this piece of art to my worship classes, the students cannot see the title. I ask them to tell me what they see. Their re-sponses range from a galaxy, to a lariat, to a child in a mother's womb, to a mother holding a child, to (and this is my favorite) the famous Muppet, Kermit the Frog, tilting his head. "We may, in our worship planning and leading," I tell my students, "set out to present an image of the Mother and Child. Toward that end we may pray, plan, research, craft, and nuance our prayers, songs, readings, ser-mons and other elements of our particular liturgy, but if we understand and approach worship correctly, authentically, we must live with the possibility that someone will see Kermit the Frog in-stead." By the way, I purchased the Betty Wood piece for its intrigue as well as its irony.

The lesson I attempt to convey is that worship planning from the first idea to the final amen is an exercise in crafting and presenting an image under the guidance of the Holy Spirit while leaving the receiv-ing, processing, and application of that image to the Holy Spirit, as well. Images created by words and susceptible to interpretation are crucial to worship. That leads us to consider the sermon.

THE SERMON

The sermon is a weaving together of journeys: the life journey of the preacher, the life journey of the hearer, and their combined jour-neys into the truth of scripture and the mysteries of God. The sermon is about listening. The pastor listens as the Holy Spirit whis-pers through God's Holy Word, the Bible. The worshipers listen to the spoken words of the pastor hoping to hear the Holy Spirit's voice. The sermon is about receiving.

I shall never forget the occasion of preparing and preaching my first (real) sermon. It was a humbling experience to know and see that the sermon did not originate in me. It came to me, required something of me, gave something to me, and flowed through me. I likened it, at the time, to standing at the bottom of a waterfall. The water was falling on me from above with great force. It was drenching me, covering me, and taking my breath away. It then moved on to its intended end, people waiting in thirst that only the Holy Spirit could quench. I came out of it feeling like I had been newly baptized.

Opening up to the sermon is first the work of the preacher, but it finally becomes the work of the people to open themselves to the same flow. The crafting of the words and the insights of a sermon are often disdained as striving too much for art and oratory. A far better way to think about the crafting and insight and, yes, the poetry of a sermon is to see such care and nuance as an exploration and a detailed record of that exploration. The sermon is an attempt to describe discoveries and thoughts that are delicate and perhaps crucial, intriguing and inviting, in a way that allows the hearers to make the same discovery for themselves; being led to the find, instead of being told about it. Crafting of words is an attempt to pass along the discoveries without detracting from them or in some other way dulling their glow.

One wants the sermon to be the occasion for the listener to hear the same whisper of the Spirit that the preacher heard in study. When that whisper is heard, the words bring the proclaimer and the people to their knees. Great oratory only brings us to our feet. The crafting of words of which we speak is evidence of a humble encounter with a great mystery, reported as honestly as possible. In situations like that, each word matters.

The exploration, discovery, and study, of course, take place within the pages of the Bible. There one detects the closest thing the Holy Spirit has to a pulse. The Spirit's life is detected in the vitality of scripture. You have heard it said, "Each time I read the scripture, it is new." The inspiration continues to reveal, because the inspiration is a person, a pulse, not an impulse. The sermon invites us to see and hear and feel the evidence of life, the life of the Holy Spirit. The life detected in the sermon is not the result of crafting words around mined insights, it is the source. The sermon and the other elements of the worship plan are in dialogue with each other; a dialogue facilitated by the Holy Spirit.

Many, not all, but many will enter worship through this door.

READINGS

Christ-followers over the years, across Christian traditions, and around the world have recorded, in written form, profound insights into God's Word and into the challenges of the life of discipleship. Many of these are quite helpful as we attempt, in our time and place, to express our worship in spirit and truth. In the Bible we encounter inspiration. In the writings of the desert fathers and mothers and religious leaders of more recent times, we encounter insight. Inspiration and insight are related in that both are the work of the Holy Spirit, but they are not synonymous. The word "readings", in this context is used to categorize sentences or paragraphs selected from essays and books by women and men whose walk with the Lord was/is a bit closer than ours, either for a lifetime or a moment.

The fragments of the larger works are selected and contemplated because the insight they reveal connects with our souls, becoming our insight as well. We "see" what the writer "saw," and our understanding of some divine mystery is deepened. These words need to be made available to the worshiper, presented as doors through which some will enter into the worship experience at hand.

Two hesitancies often surface in discussions about the use of readings in worship. One concern gathers around the idea that the time, space, and focus given to readings could be better invested in scripture itself. The other flag of caution is this: What if the person being quoted is discovered to have had some sort of moral deficiency or breakdown that could embarrass or distract worshipers if found out? The first hesitancy should be met with the inspiration/insight criteria put forth in the previous paragraph. The Holy Spirit is at work revealing insights. Indeed, written insights are quite similar to spoken "testimonies" of God's hand at work in our lives. Testimonies are welcomed in the worship of a number of Christian traditions. Insight into life is an important aspect of worship. Readings simply bridge a time gap, bringing great testimonies into the present. Readings are similar to hymns, just without the musical notes.

There was a time when we might have compared readings of this sort to notes left on the spiritual refrigerator door. But technology is changing our language and images, along with just about everything else. Now it would probably be more up to date to say that readings are text messages from Christ-followers of long ago.

The second hesitancy, the one concerning the moral consistency of the writers, must not be applied narrowly. Indeed, the writers of "readings" represent a risk to the holiness of worship. But, alas, so do the writers of hymns and composers of hymn tunes. The biggest consideration at this point, of course, is that God chose to bring scripture to us through the pens of human writers. There is no lack of shady characters in that bunch. If we want sin-free writers, planners, and leaders for our worship, we are in trouble. But, thanks be to God, our scripture, sermons, songs, and readings, flowing through human imperfection, pass through the filters of redemption, forgiveness, and grace. Further, our worship planners and leaders are forgiven sinners saved by grace. Readings, as an element of worship, are just fresh enough to be good reminders of the place God has given the human element in divine worship. Redemption, forgiveness, and grace are important aspects of worship.

We should receive sermons, sing psalms, hymns, and spiritual songs, and contemplate "readings" with peace of heart and mind. God knows us all, loves us all, inspires us all at different times and in differing ways, whether we recognize it or not, and invites us all to worship, stumble as we might as we enter the sanctuary.

LITANIES

Worship is a dialogue. It is a conversation that God initiates. We acknowledge this truth about worship when we engage in litanies, responsive readings, and antiphonal readings because worship, itself, is a litany of sorts. God initiates, we respond. God speaks, we speak or sing or pray. Grace is offered, we accept. God transcends, we are transformed. Litanies reflect worship's conversation or dialogue. Litanies create a rhythm of listening and responding, and a sort of breathing (inhaling and exhaling) in the life of worship.

For many worshipers, litanies are "old hat," familiar methods of participation in worship. For many other worshipers, though, the word "litany" is unusual and a bit foreign. The closest thing to litany that they have encountered is the responsive reading of scripture, in a bold-print/light-print format located in the back of their hymnal. "Litany," both the word and the format, can seem a bit too formal in a tradition such as this. If this sense of uncertainty exists in your congregation, you might consider the fact that litanies give worshipers the experience of hearing the right words come out of their mouth. It is a sample of what right thoughts and right words feel like, as well as sound like, coming from "me" and "us." If that seems somewhat presumptuous or even manipulative, consider litanies as examples or models or templates for rehearsing desired responses to the truths and challenges of God's word. Let the congregation know they are invited, not required to participate in these patterns that for some are prayer and for others, practice. The truth is that litanies are no more prescriptive than are hymns or any other type of congregational song or even prayers to which the congregation says, "Amen." Things are sung or said or prayed on behalf of the congregation in all Christian traditions.

Litanies help bring about focus and a sense of community. Worshipers can be "taken by the hand" through the use of a litany, and "ushered" into worship, gently and corporately. Participation is easy and the words are, quite often, conversational. The subject of a good litany is obvious and timely.

Litanies allow persons other than the pastor to exercise leadership in worship. This is important in free-church, congregational settings. For all their prescribed words, litanies are quite congregational, democratic, and friendly to the concept of the priesthood of the believer. Litanies carry the weight of the sound of the congregation in unison. There is depth in that sound, and solidarity. The sound and its message become three dimensional as the congregation gives voice and face and spirit to the words.

PRAYERS

Prayers load and stretch our words to the maximum. Praying is the hardest work our words ever do. Confessing our sin, praising our Maker and Redeemer, pouring our hearts out for loved ones, begging for understanding in times of tragedy; this is the stuff of prayer and the most severe test of the strength and capacity of our words.

Differences of opinion concerning spontaneous prayer and prepared or pre-existing prayers have fueled discussion and debate for centuries. This little book does not end the dialogue. It simply tugs at the shirttails of the deeper and wiser voices.

The criterion for prayer should be that it is the sincere utterance of the soul. Spontaneity does not insure sincerity. Neither do time nor bookbinding defeat sincerity. There is something about the human heart and mind that makes some prayers relevant in any and every age. Prayers for peace come to mind immediately. "Yes, that is what I wanted to say." "Those are our words, exactly." Such responses are evidence that carefully considered prayers are, indeed, authentic and sincere, and can be a meaningful ministry to the congregation.

The oft heard, "Bless the gift and the giver," is a phrase that is frequently the brunt of insider church jokes. But, when one thinks of the timelessness of that prayer, it can be seen as a prayer for the ages that just has not been written down yet. Those words will be authentic and timely as long as Christ-followers gather to worship and understand collecting money to share with others as being Biblical and an act of worship. It is both a request and an acknowledgement. We know that giving is blessed by God, and we ask that it continue to be blessed by God. There is also the hope of the loaves and fishes in that prayer. "Lord, this is what we have to give today. It comes from you, and we return it in your name. Let us see the miracle that only you can bring about; abundance, not in our pockets, but in the meeting of the needs of the world." In short, "Bless the gift and the giver."

Written, pre-composed prayers present a pattern and create community. One need only consider Jesus' model prayer ("The Lord's Prayer" or "Our Father") to see indisputable evidence of this. People who know nothing else about Christianity may well know this prayer which is prayed by all who call themselves Christ-followers. True, it was first prayed by Jesus, himself, and it is scripture. But prayers that are not also scripture have found their way through the ages, born in the hearts and on the backs of the faithful who have found their words inspiring in those circumstances common to all humans.

Time does not alter the sincerity of a prayer of thanksgiving for rain that breaks a drought. God exists in the eternal now, and human need will be here as long as humans are here. Time is not an issue. Sincerity is the issue. Authenticity is crucial.

Some in the congregation will consciously enter into worship when the prayer being prayed is the deep expression of their heart. It will not matter to them whether it was written last century, last night, or it was spontaneous. The prayer was their words, shared at some time and place by another human being in the same state of heart and mind. They enter worship there. They could enter worship at no other time or place on this day, and the prayer was there for them.

The prayer was breathed into their worship for that day, and they were able to breathe it out as their own and the inhaling and exhaling of that prayer was the very breath of life for that worshiper on that day and for days to come. So much more was planned and available. So many others entered into worship at other portals, but this prayer on this day matched this person's need. That is a God thing, as "they" say. It is the work of the Holy Spirit, across barriers of time and space.

Finding corporate prayers that express the heart cries of your congregation can only be accomplished as you learn those hearts. It becomes obvious to the worshiper that the one who selected the prayers for today, knows me.

Appropriate corporate prayers, pre-existing or spontaneous, are as close to the people as are the "prayers of the people" which are common in many traditions. The prayers of the people are a directed focus that exists on a continuum, somewhere between pre-existing prayer and spontaneous prayer in terms of their origin.

The point is to present an opening for authentic participation in worship, acknowledging that "lockstep" entrance into, and involvement in, worship is neither possible nor desirable.

LANGUAGE ISSUES

As worship planners, we must take care that our words say what we intend for them to say. We may not like it when the meanings of words change, but we cannot ignore those changes. We must consider how the words of worship will be heard and how they will function. We must know the importance of the words we want to go to the worshipers and the words we want to come from the worshipers. We must make every effort to insure that the words received and expressed are the words of holy conversation, inspired in their coming and going, in their weaving of heart to heart.

In the English language, we do not have formal and informal pronouns. Attitudes and inflection can show respect for a person or the lack of it, but in the written word, it is hard to establish the attitude behind the word "You." Because of that, "church language" has picked up on the formal sound of pronouns in what has become known as "King James English." Thee, Thy, and Thou sound more formal, perhaps, more respectful, even though they are not used in any level of conversation. What sounds to some as formal and respectful, sounds to others as archaic, aloof, or simply questionable: "Why are they talking like that?"

Another language issue is that of words that cause people to feel excluded rather than included. The use of "man" to mean all people is no longer universally accepted or understood in that way. The word's meaning has changed whether we like it or not. When we are admonished to "stand up for Jesus" some are excluded...not because of their lack of commitment, but because of their lack of the physical capacity to stand. What does it mean to people of dark skin when the work of Christ is seen as "washing" away our dark sin in order to make us "whiter than snow." [2]

What of militaristic language? We are, indeed, involved in spiritual warfare (Ephesians 6: 10-17). Paul admonishes us in scripture to put on the full armor of God because of that warfare. Those words, however, refuse to stay confined to spiritual matters in a world such as ours today. "Onward, Christian soldiers, marching as to war"[3] shouts against official statements that the war on terror is not a war on Islam. We know the intent and parameters of the hymn and the war, but many will not (not even all those within the Church).

As was stated at the beginning of this chapter, words matter. The definitions and usage of words change. We cannot ignore these characteristics of words if it is important that our worship be characterized by spirit and truth in its hearing as well as in its intent.

---

[2] Hymn "Whiter than Snow." Words, James Nicholson (c.1828-1876); Music William G. Fishcher (1835-1912).

[3] Hymn "Onward, Christian Soldiers." Words, Sabine Baring-Gould (1834-1924); Music, Arthur S. Sullivan (1842-1900)

But the hour is coming, and is now here, when the true worshippers will worship the Father in spirit and truth, for the Father seeks such as these to worship him. God is spirit, and those who worship him must worship in spirit and truth.' (John 4: 23-24)

Everyone who reads these pages is no doubt quite aware of these language issues. The issues are not new, even though they remain current. They are reviewed here simply as a reminder of the responsibility of the worship planner, especially at the point of words in worship.

In a very real sense, all the words of worship constitute a language issue. We must see God's Holy Word, the Bible, as words that speak truth against the lies of evil and destruction. We must use words that tell the truth about God and pull us into the greater mystery of God's love. We must use words that tell the truth of human struggle and weakness. We must use the words of our prose until only poetry can carry the load, and then the words of our poetry must give way to spiritual utterances in silent prayer.

Many people will enter into worship through worship's words. They will listen for the poetry that lifts like earth-born mists of prayer to meet with Heaven-bound clouds of praise. They will listen for the engagement of real life prose with God's real words of forgiveness, hope, and promise. That is where many will stand and listen before they enter into worship.

Worship planners/leaders know that words must be handled as if they were explosive. Words must be handled as if they were sharp. Words must be handled as if they were fragile. Words must be handled as if they were priceless. Words must be handled as if they were keys that unlocked the heavy doors of a life sentence. Words must be handled as if they contained the world's only hope. Words must be handled as if they were the hinges that allow the doors of worship to swing both ways.

CHAPTER THREE

Entering Through Music

Now, as then, music summons God's people to worship.

Stars hovered over the tents as they did every night–Abraham's blessing resting high above the camp. The desert darkness would soon surrender to the rose-pink advance of twilight; but for now, in this protected moment, earth was reconciled with heaven and all was at peace.

Against the predawn slumber, a voice came calling, shattering the stillness, reaching deep into every mountain crevice and trumpeting down to the valley below. The sheep answered back with a cacophony of bleating as if to greet it both with expectation and dread. The high, urgent blasts pierced Rachel's dreams. "Not now," she thought. "The night has been too short, my body too weary." Little Reuben clutched her tightly about the waist and buried his head in her side. "Abba's tales of Egyptian chariots and horsemen are a mistake at this tender age." Rousing herself, she sat up. Above her, Simon's muscular form moved about, reaching for his sash, girding it about his tunic. This early rising was expected. He and Abba must be among the first men at the gate. "But where is Abba? He would not have left Simon behind...would he?" Rachel's eyes darted about, then rested on the tent opening which framed a dark silhouette with arms raised toward the sky–Abba joining in reunion with Ima, the patriarchs, and God.

"Life is treacherous but good," thought Rachel, then she whispered, "Jehovah provides."

Closing her still heavy eyelids, she prayed that the moment might become eternity. But the song of the morning trumpets continued; preparations had been made; the feast would begin.

> The Lord spoke to Moses, saying: Make two silver trumpets; you shall make them of hammered work; and you shall use them for summoning the congregation, and for breaking camp. When both are blown, the whole congregation shall assemble before you at the entrance of the tent of meeting... Also on your days of rejoicing, at your appointed festivals, and at the beginnings of your months, you shall blow the trumpets over your burnt offerings and over your sacrifices of well-being; they shall serve as a reminder on your behalf before the Lord your God: I am the Lord your God. (Numbers 10:1-4, 10 NRSV)

The silver trumpets summoned the Hebrew congregation to its place of worship. Their song could be heard by all, but how it was heard varied from person to person. Some heard it as a commandment and others as an invitation. To some the trumpet song announced a celebration but to others impending doom. Everyone, however, knew their duty to respond though the responses were not all the same.

Abba and Simon passed through the flocks looking for a lamb. Simon had dreaded this moment for he already knew what the choice must be. This lamb must be perfect–no defect or even a blemish. Recalling Abraham and Isaac on Mount Moriah, he surveyed the flocks, anxiously in search of another possibility.

Abba said, "It must be done."

Simon pushed his way through the flock, stopped, reached down and then hoisted to his shoulders the prize lamb. He turned, nodded, and with the breaking dawn he and Abba made their way to the tent of meeting carrying the sacrifice. The trumpets blew.

The priest summoned the two inside the tabernacle door to receive the morning sacrifice. As the lamb was led to the altar, Abba sighed. The sacrifice meant life and prosperity for his people, his daughter, and her family. But Simon, could not bring himself to look...Reuben's pet lamb taken to the slaughter. What would he say to his son when they visited the flocks, and it was gone? What can a child be told about sin and the spilling of blood?

The trumpets played; the sacrifice was made.

Now, as then, music summons God's people to worship. Unlike Old Testament times, however, there is no tabernacle, no altar of burnt offering, no holy of holies. God is with us, revealed in Christ Jesus and indwelling the church through the Spirit's presence. We are still called to worship, and still we enter worship with a myriad of emotions accompanying the calling and entrance. They vary between individual worshipers, depending on life's situation. A "Simon" may feel sorrow, while an "Abba" feels satisfaction. Over time, feelings easily attach themselves to songs and are triggered when the songs are sung. This phenomenon may even be misidentified as worship itself. Have you ever heard someone say "the music just didn't help me worship today"? Truly, worship and its music are connected to the emotions. Consider the verse "I will be glad and exult in you; I will sing praise to your name, O Most High." (Psalm 9:2 NRSV). It must also be acknowledged, however, that music can make us glad at movies, concerts, and sporting events; and one can remain unrepentant and unconnected with God and His people while listening to the most appealing musical presentations in church.

The trumpets sound, and the songs are sung not to conjure up a response, but to accompany the response occurring within each hearer. Often, though, church music is not understood or practiced in this way. Consider the pastor who requests that all service music be in a major key because the minor creates too melancholy a mood; or the music minister who will not teach the congregation new hymns because of the emotional attachment the people have to the old.

There are problems with those ways of thinking. It assumes all people respond in the same way, and that spiritual outcomes can be programmed with the right kind of music. It also assumes that people remain the same; that their response today will be the same tomorrow; that there is no real growth, no development, and no change. Finally, it reduces worship planning to temporal rather than eternal considerations measuring success by pulling the right strings of the members; or as a guest to a service once said "they kept trying to do things to me!"

The goal is not to worship in the song but to pass through the song into worship. The song is analogous to the tabernacle entrance in the same way the heart is to the altar. In true worship, the song is only the doorway to the heart. Nevertheless, choices must be made about songs for services to be planned. Rather than tell us how fast or slow the music must be or how high or low it should be sung, scripture offers precepts to guide our planning. In this chapter we will consider three; they are:

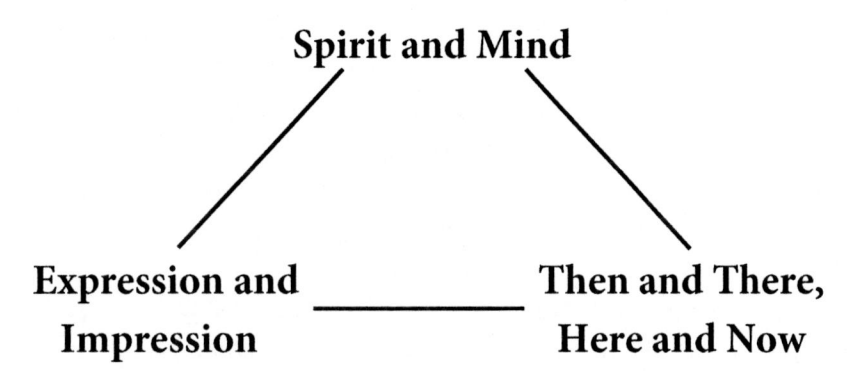

Spirit and Mind

Expression and Impression   **Then and There, Here and Now**

SPIRIT AND MIND

> "A time is coming and has now come when the true worshipers will worship the Father in spirit and truth, for they are the kind of worshippers the Father seeks. God is spirit, and his worshipers must worship in spirit and in truth." (John 4:23-24 NIV)

Have you noticed how Jesus never talked about song selection, major and minor modes, and old hymns versus new? Such things, along with the place and time of worship, Jesus dismissed as unimportant compared to the one requirement of worshipping the Father in spirit and truth. There is an obvious Trinitarian reference here— the spirit being the Holy Spirit, the truth being the Son with each doing their work to bring worshippers to the Father. There is also a connection to the human dimensions of spirit and mind.

The spirit is the breath of life breathed into Adam's nostrils at creation. It is the force that animates and causes us to seek the Creator and enjoy His creation. With the mind we think, reason, form opinions, and come to understand the truth. God tells us that His Spirit bears witness with our spirits that we are His children.

> For all who are led by the Spirit of God are children of God. For you did not receive a spirit of slavery to fall back into fear, but you have received a spirit of adoption. When we cry, 'Abba! Father!' it is that very Spirit bearing witness with our spirit that we are children of God. (Romans 8:14-16)

We are also told that in worship, our minds are to be renewed.

> I appeal to you therefore, brothers and sisters, by the mercies of God, to present your bodies as a living sacrifice, holy and acceptable to God, which is your spiritual worship. (Romans 12:1)

It is the Holy Spirit that helps our minds to understand the truth, and it is the truth that bridles our spirits into submission to Him.

All this is important to song selection, for congregations vary in the relative importance they attach to the dimensions of mind and spirit. This variety of opinion also exists within a congregation. One member of the "mind first" persuasion says "I'm just not being fed." A "spirit first" member remarks, "the service isn't charging me up."

The "mind first" worshiper is concerned with the theology and practice of worship. She enjoys a deep, thoughtful exposition of God's word and an ordered service in which all the elements tie together around a central truth. She finds lighthearted comments between songs to be unnecessary and in poor taste. The church calendar is meaningful with its observances of Lent, Advent, and Easter along with special emphases that communicate the congregation's mission and ministry. Tradition and recollections of the congregation's history provide rich context for its expressions of faith.

The "spirit first" worshiper speaks of the worship "experience." He longs for a move of God's Spirit among the members of the congregation. Jovial pulpit personalities, testimonies of God's provision, Bible preaching that calls for public decision, fervent prayer, loud exuberant praise, to him, are among the life signs of a vibrant congregation.

Once when preparing the music for an occasion where a celebrated preacher was to speak, I asked his associate what the sermon text would be, explaining that the information would help in my song selection. The associate replied, "It doesn't matter. Just pump the people up and turn them over." This statement represents a "spirit first" (or spirit only) approach to church music. How unlike the Old Testament prophets who sang their prophecy. They sang not to "pump the people up" but to confront them with the truth of God's word even if that word would be deflating. Church music is often evaluated according to how it makes one feel rather than what it calls one to consider.

Music can and should touch the spirit! Remember how King Saul's spirit was soothed with the music from David's harp? Remember David's exuberant dance before the Ark of the Covenant? May every congregation have music that both soothes and quickens its spirit. Let us be careful here, however. The spirit can also be stirred by music with no worship association. You can get "pumped" from the music at a rock concert or a basketball game! Worship music, though, is music through which God's Spirit bears witness with our spirits to the end that our minds are renewed. To settle for less would be no more edifying than the ranting of Baal's prophets as they attempted to call down fire from Heaven. The Apostle Paul had it right.

> I will pray with the spirit and I will pray with the mind also; I will sing with the spirit and I will sing with the mind also. (1 Corinthians 14:15)

Songs should move the spirit, but they should also help the mind consider the truth. Considering the truth means that we will sometimes ponder that which is not easily understood or communicated by our favorite musical style. It will mean that we will learn new songs along with singing the ones we already know. It will mean that the songs will teach us even as does the preacher's message. It means that we will bequeath to our children not only the current hits but also the songs that will bear witness throughout their lives of God's goodness and grace.

IMPRESSION AND EXPRESSION

In a service, there are times of inner contemplation, times to outwardly demonstrate one's worship, and times when one can do both. The themes of impression and expression run the course of scripture as in this verse where both appear.

> "Be still, and know that I am God; I will be exalted among the nations, I will be exalted in the earth." (Psalm 46:10)

"Be still, and know" are acts of impression; "exalt" is an act of expression. (Maybe being still is also an expressive act.)

Kent sings enthusiastically with the congregation "Rejoice, the Lord is King." The hymn has been one of his favorites since he learned it in chapel services during the short time he attended seminary. "What ever happened to that idealistic young man and the call?" he wonders. Jennifer sits silently in the row before him. She does not know this song and ponders the lyrics as Kent sings. "Rejoice?" she questions. "There's too much heartache for that." Later, though, when "Speak, O Lord" is sung, Jennifer does join in. She comes close to tears whenever the song is used, but this morning it is the cry of her heart for comfort and direction. Behind her, Kent sits silently listening again for the call, praying that God will speak.

This impression/expression dynamic was set in motion long before Kent and Jennifer entered the room. It began when someone read God's word, lived it, and expressed it as poetry. The poetry impressed itself upon a composer and became music. The worship planner considered scripture, poetry and music against the impressions she had about her congregation. She expressed herself (or a group of planners themselves) in a service plan which was offered to the congregation. The congregation followed the plan, and in response to the impressions received, expressed itself silently to God and through singing with one another.

To put it simply, hearing something new brings to mind something old, and when the two are joined, a new impression is born which in turn finds its expression. Thus, a worship service is not a narrow restatement of the same point through songs, readings, and a sermon, but the gradual revealing of a broader truth applied in unseen ways among a congregation's many members.

THEN AND THERE, HERE AND NOW

> *In Christ there is no East or West,*
> *In Him no South or North;*
> *But one great fellowship of love*
> *Throughout the whole wide earth.*
>
> *-William A. Dunkerley, 1908*

All the songs ever written cannot fully explore the depth of human emotion, nor can all the songs yet to be. As long as human beings share life experiences with their joys and heartaches–as long as they know both gain and loss–they will share their songs, for through them they join in an expression of spirit in search of truth.

Through song, Christians can enter together into worship. This union occurs within a local congregation and in a larger fellowship among congregations gathered "throughout the whole wide earth." Their togetherness is revealed in a hymnody enveloping expressions of different lands and times. Chinese congregations sing the nineteenth century English hymn "Holy, Holy, Holy" as do congregations in the American south. Even the most provincial church members unknowingly belt out tunes from all over the world, considering the hymns to be their own.

The inheritance of past texts and tunes from around the world also connects a congregation with the great company of saints who now worship in Heaven. Attachments are strong to the songs daddy and momma sang and their parents before them. To sing these songs is to commune with the saints and to be reminded of the truths they taught us. Family connections, however, are not the only reason why songs from then and there impact the here and now.

The songs have impact because they have meaning. A beautiful, singable tune united with a strong, moving text will continue to make an impression upon the listener and become a vehicle for expression no matter when or where it was written. Time passes along the best of these songs to us. We connect with them because they convey the elemental aspects of human experience in relation to God and His world. The circumstances of our experience will vary based on our age, where we live, our race, and many other factors, but the hunger for God at the root of all experience is the same. An elderly person and a teenager can join together in the singing of "Amazing Grace", though the application of grace in each of their lives is different.

The psalmist said about his song "Let this be written for a future generation, that a people not yet created may praise the LORD"

(Psalm 102:18 NIV). In like manner, each generation has the sacred duty of writing and discovering hymns of the here and now to add to the inheritance given to it from the past, the then and there. These new songs may come from the popular songs of young adulthood or songs written in the tradition of classical hymnody. They may include old texts set to new tunes or new settings of old tunes. They should include songs of many nations for no nation has a monopoly on spirit and truth. Writing and discovering these new treasures is not enough, however. The songs must be launched if they are to reach a "people not yet created." They are launched by their singing. In learning and singing them, we draw closer to God and to one another, and we join in worship with Christians who will come after us. Our songs of the here and now become their songs of the then and there.

ENTERING THROUGH THE SONG

> *Let us sing alleluia here on earth, while we still live in anxiety, so that we may sing it one day in heaven in full security...* –Augustine

Songs are the entryway into the tabernacle where living sacrifices are made. Through the interplay of the dynamics presented above, the members of your congregation will find the tent opening and move into and through the Worship Matrix. They will sing songs they have known all their lives and songs that are new to them that morning. They will sing simple songs with spirit and songs which demand a consideration of the truth. They will express their praise with abandon and soak up the many impressions that come from hearing the congregation's voice. Some of their songs could be described as "mind expressions of the here and now" and others "spirit impressions of the then and there." Finally, they will carry their songs into life singing an "alleluia" on earth knowing that one day it will be sung in Heaven.

The ceremony ended. Abba and Simon turned from the tabernacle to make the slow, silent trip back home. They knew this would not be the last journey. One day, too soon, it would be Reuben's responsibility to carry the lamb and then his sons and theirs after. What they knew came to be. The trumpets did play over and over again until a day on a rocky hillside when the sacrifice itself sang the song. "Why have you forsaken me?"–Simon's song of sorrow. "It is finished..."–Abba's song of accomplishment.

To the sound of the trumpets and the cry of Golgotha, we sing.

CHAPTER FOUR

Entering Through the Fellowship

An ice-breaker at a party only serves to help the introverts and extroverts identify each other, it doesn't "cure them." That is also true in worship if the "time of greeting" is the only conscious attempt at creating fellowship. Fellowship is created when the readings touch and unite the souls present, when the litanies uncover common ground, and when the sermon touches on life's realities and Heaven's hope. Fellowship of this sort, community on this level, is the point of entry into worship for a number of people.

The book you hold in your hands was written by two introverts. So anything said here about fellowship can be taken as the solid truth; no frills.

Loneliness is an ironic epidemic in our crowded and busy society. It can be crippling and is often the cause of depression. The fellowship of a congregation may be the life-giving entry point into worship for a lonely person. It is their entrance into the matrix of worship that not only brings companionship for the journey, but the purpose and the energy of being needed, as well.

Further, fellowship creates an environment of trust. Sadly, trust is eroding in many aspects of society. Identity theft, loss of what was thought to be safely invested money, abuse of every sort by clergy, and other breaches of trust leave one cautious about reaching out or joining anything. All this makes the safe and nurturing fellowship aspect of Christian worship extremely important.

GATHERING FOR WORSHIP

Gathering for worship is an act of worship in and of itself. It is a political statement. Not a democrat vs. republican political statement. Gathering for worship is a Kingdom of Heaven vs. the Kingdom of this World political statement. As we gather we declare that first and foremost, our citizenship is in Heaven and that Jesus is Lord. There are some in our world for whom this act of worship puts their very lives at risk. Even so, they gather. This is fellowship that matters. This is an indication of the power and importance of Christian fellowship. Indeed, worship should bring each of us ever closer to daily dying to self, but for some it has physical implications.

The fellowship of worship is a gathering of brothers and sisters who need each other in the face of spiritual warfare, and who encourage each other in the face of real or potential persecution. This fact, alone, should cause us to protect and cultivate the importance of fellowship and community. Let us pray and say and sing "we" far more than "I." Let us pass the peace of Christ by one method or other as an oath of allegiance to him and to each other. And let us welcome the stranger, not out of benevolence, but out of respect and awe for this possible angel. Let us welcome the stranger knowing that he or she might even be Jesus, come to bless our fellowship as he blessed the wedding at Cana. Let our fellowship bless the stranger as we remember the importance of sharing a cup of water (Matthew 10:42), clothing, and food (Matthew 25: 31-46). Fellowship, itself, is made holy by these possibilities.

Gathering for worship is a family reunion. The terms brother and sister are still prominent in many Christian traditions and communities. It is a beautiful practice to greet each other in this way. It declares the gathering to be deep and vital and binding. The words "sister" and "brother" put congregational relationships in a special perspective of responsibility to each other.

No congregation or family is perfect. Some are dysfunctional. But in many, perhaps most, cases, a family gathering brings with it refreshing memories and moments of hope. Family strengthens us for the realities of life, allowing us to see and study those realities in a familiar microcosm. Gathered in reunion, family says here is your heritage and hope; here is your place and your courage in the present reality. For many people, fellowship that is as close or nearly as close as family is their entry point into worship. Worship planners and leaders must know this and cultivate the implications of the truth of it.

INTROVERTS AND EXTROVERTS

Sharing thoughts in the context of this heading brings a smile. The fellowship aspect of worship saves both introverts and extroverts from themselves. Jesus fed the five thousand after they had flocked to him and after the disciples had advised him to send them away (Matthew 14: 13-21). Now there is an extrovert for you. But immediately after the crowd was fed, Jesus sent his disciples on ahead so that he could be alone. How alone? His solitude included taking a walk on water. Now there is an introvert for you. No one is going to bother you on that walk. Well, some extrovert might try it. (Matthew 14: 22-33)

Fellowship encourages being present to each other. Jesus is in the crowd. He heals the blind, whether they cannot see because they look away, or whether they can only see themselves. Introverts who might look away from the other person, and extroverts who might only see the other person in light of themselves will fail to see Jesus present in that person. The fellowship present in worship can be used by God to heal this blindness. The fellowship of worship can, indeed, bring us to the point of seeing Jesus in others. It may also help us believe that it is possible for Jesus to be seen in us.

Jesus is Lord of everyone who will declare it; introverts, extroverts, and everyone in between. Jesus is their Lord and is with them in their crowd or in their corner. Fellowship that facilitates each seeing the Christ in the other can be the entryway into worship.

Jesus also prayed that his followers, those in the front and those in the back, would be one (John 17). Fellowship brings this about. The fellowship of worship brings about an oneness through submission and obedience and a communal identity. Having one service for the extroverts and another for the introverts is a strange response to Jesus' prayer. Dying to self for the sake of the other is an appropriate, sacrificial response and act of worship. It is also an act of fellowship.

That an ice-breaker at a party only serves to help the introverts and the extroverts identify each other, it doesn't "cure" them, is also true in worship if the "time of greeting" is the only conscious attempt at creating fellowship. Fellowship is created when the readings touch and unite the souls present, when the litanies uncover common ground, and when the sermon touches on life's realities and Heaven's hope. Fellowship of this sort, community on this level, is the point of entry into worship for a number of people.

In the context of introverts, extroverts and the fellowship of worship, two seemingly contradictory passages of scripture take on new meaning. "Make a joyful noise" (Psalm 66: 1, et al.) and "Keep silence" (Habakkuk 2:20 et al.) have been used to justify both separate worship services and blended worship services. Could it be possible that these two admonitions, taken together, call introverts and extroverts, respectively, to learn from each other and to minister to each other in the context of worshiping together? If so, the worship planner/leader should be mindful of this; not settling for blending musical styles for the sake of keeping the peace, but doing the work of employing the dynamics of fellowship to bring about obedience, submission, and sacrifice in worship.

A Cloud of Witnesses

Hebrews 12: 1 gives us an interesting place to stand to consider the fellowship aspects of worship.

> Therefore, since we are surrounded by so great a cloud of witnesses, let us also lay aside every weight and the sin that clings to closely, and let us run with perseverance the race that is set before us, looking to Jesus the pioneer and perfecter of our faith, who for the sake of the joy that was set before him endured the cross, disregarding its shame, and has taken his seat at the right hand of the throne of God. (NRSV)

When we gather to worship, we are encouraged by those present. We see that we are not alone in our allegiance to Christ, in Christian worship, nor in our efforts toward discipleship throughout the week. Indeed, the fellowship of worship creates a cloud of witnesses for a lifetime of worship and discipleship. A helpful insight here is that, "It is what the runner sees in the witnesses, not what the witnesses see in the runner, that inspires him."[4] We have long known that worship is inspiring, even though that is not the purpose of worship. Our worship is not directed toward the witnesses for their approval, but being with others in worship is encouraging. Worship is to God and for God, but the inspiration of the worshiper is a wonderful by-product of worship.

This passage of scripture from Hebrews helps us understand how fellowship functions in the process of the worshiper being inspired. Certainly the worshiper is inspired by the work of the Holy Spirit who enables our worship. But the idea that we are inspired, as well, by fellowship with those present brings a sort of weightiness to show-

---

[4] Charles A. Trentham, "Hebrews," in *The Broadman Bible Commentary* (ed. Clifton J. Allen; vol. 12 *Hebrews-Revelation General Articles*, ed. John William MacGorman and Frank Stagg; Nashville: Broadman Press, 1972), 85.

ing up and participating in worship. Fellowship means that we are ministering to each other as we worship God. It also sheds new light on the importance of cross-generational worship. Fellowship of a cross-generational nature broadens our view of those whose lives can encourage and inspire us. We can receive inspiration and encouragement from those who are older than us and those who are younger than us, whether we are speaking of age or time as a Christ-follower. Cross-generational worship provides a full-orbed cloud of witnesses, not just a crowd of people whose age and experience mirrors ours.

A PREVIEW OF HEAVEN

Will Heaven be hell if the music there is not my style? It is a shocking question, and in fact is included here, in part, because of its shock value, as well as the perspective it brings. When one thinks of fellowship in the presence of Jesus, the thought and the image force earthly concerns and issues out of the picture. It will be the fellowship that makes it heaven; fellowship with Jesus first and foremost, then fellowship with the redeemed, as well. What music will we sing there? It seems self-centered to ask. It is an earth born and earth bound question.

One pauses at the thought that music might be subservient to fellowship. At least musicians pause, and we can imagine that most other worship planners and leaders would as well. Could fellowship really be that important? Imagine being in the presence of Jesus, totally focused on him and what it means to be in his presence. Then imagine a situation in which being together is more important than singing, and singing together is more important than the songs.

An unsettling thought occurs. The imaginings just suggested in the paragraph above might describe worship in the "underground" or marginalized church on earth as readily as it describes worship in Heaven. It should describe all Christian worship. Even though we claim it is for God and for authenticity, worshiping in our preferred style is a luxury we lavish on ourselves when our situation will allow it. Folks worshiping "underground" or on the "margins" of society do not have that luxury, yet their worship might be more like that in Heaven than any other here on earth: being together more important than singing, singing together more important than the songs. It is possible that we have discovered both the quality of fellowship and the cost of devotion that characterize authentic worship in any circumstance. The quality of fellowship: Jesus at the head of it all and in the midst of it all. The cost of devotion: the sacrifice of Jesus on the cross and the worshiper on the margin.

It has often been said that worship here on earth is rehearsal for worship in Heaven. That bit of liturgical theology may have a few holes in it, but the idea is not totally off base. Perhaps, though, it is more accurate to think in terms of our worship on earth joining that of Heaven. To the extent that is true, we must concern ourselves with the quality of fellowship and devotion engendered by the worship we plan and lead.

Holding Heaven in our hearts and minds will bring hope and joy to our worship. Equally as important, it will also bring to our worship new levels of humility in terms of devotion and fellowship. Earth's realities and Heaven's realities meet in Christian worship. Our fellowship is one of helping each other navigate our dual citizenship, our struggle and our hope, our spiritual and physical oneness. When this facet of our fellowship is evident, some people will be especially drawn to enter into worship through this portal. Diversity is acknowledged by which portal one chooses to enter, in this case, through unique and compelling fellowship. Unity will be found by participating in the worship that is underway when they get there.

THE FELLOWSHIP OF THE CHOIR

Choirs are being re-discovered in Contemporary Worship. Those of us who have been in the loft all along must not give in to the temptation to say, "I told you so." Rather, our response should be "Thanks be to God," because an important arena of fellowship is being restored.

Fellowship occurs within the choir and between the choir and the congregation. Within the choir, a good sense of fellowship keeps the tone quality of the singing warm and full. This is because the choir members enjoy being together and leaning on each other musically. Listening to each other's prayer requests, then praying with them, even having conversations with them in the parking lot after choir rehearsal; these are times of listening that carry over into the listening required to make well blended sounds in choral music. This is fellowship, formal and informal, but enriching either way. Worship is enriched, and for some, this warmth of fellowship is the entry point into worship. It is a gratifying thing to see people join a church while wearing a choir robe. Less noticeable, but equally important is to have people enter into worship while wearing a choir robe. Both choir members and congregation members are more attentive, whether they realize it or not, when fellowship has warmed and shaped the music. Those in the choir loft and those in the pews join each other in the fellowship of the deepened prayer and enhanced testimony of the choir's music.

Fellowship between the choir and the congregation has to do with the fact that choir members spend time with each other as family members, committee members, and Sunday School class members. These are connections that can be called upon by the worship planner and leader. This message, or that scripture passage, or this prayer will be especially meaningful to the congregation in the context of worship when it is expressed by these people, in this choir, at this time. The scripture could have been read. The prayer could have been spoken. The particular message of the anthem could have been a part of the sermon. But the unique fellowship of choir members and congregation members was activated, enhancing this particular element of worship. Perhaps it will be because of a specific musical nuance brought about by the choir and the congregation knowing each other so well (fellowship) that someone previously only present in worship actually becomes a worshiper.

I AND WE

"I" isolates. "We" connects. Fellowship requires big doses of connective language scattered throughout the service. Each of the readings, prayers, songs, and litanies in a particular worship setting should be evaluated in this regard. Indeed, our relationship to God is personal, but it is incubated, nurtured and developed in community. In like manner, our worship is personal, but it is born, encouraged, and made mature in community. In both cases our Christ-following is enhanced by community.

An over-abundance of the word "I" in corporate worship can negate all that was achieved in the act of gathering and all the blessings that are unique to community. Each time the word is said, sung, or heard, isolation is reinforced. One does not come to worship to have their loneliness validated and made more acute by a crowd.

The connective power of the word "we" will create an environment that welcomes a lonely person into community and worship. It takes at least two people to activate the word "we." The comfort of companionship is in that word. There is also the weight and energy of accountability in the word. Responsibility for each other is packed into the little word, "we."

There will be times when "I" is the appropriate positioning of what is about to be said or sung. But the careful worship planner will insert the word into the corporate worship experience sparingly and with much thought.

Fellowship is created when community is seen as a source of life and energy. "We" becomes a word and concept that warms and comforts. "We" is full of hope as it welcomes the stranger. Of course, "we" can become exclusive, even unintentionally. We have the responsibility to nurture the welcoming aspects of the word and be on guard against the exclusionary aspects of the word, especially in worship.

FELLOWSHIP ACROSS THE AGES

Increasingly, young people are becoming interested in the history and heritage of Christianity. This is seen most readily in phenomena such as the "Emerging Church" and modern worship songs that include traditional hymns wedded to new songs. In these combinations, the new song serves as commentary on the traditional hymn. In the modern worship style, traditional hymns can stand alone, but their melodies might be stretched by augmented note values and the harmonies are thinner than in the original version. Even so, there is a fellowship established and valued between the old and the new.

This growing trend of honoring the past in present day worship styles calls upon the worship planner/leader to consider songs and readings of differing sorts from ancient Christian traditions such as the writings of the "Desert Fathers and Mothers" and prayers and songs from worship books such as *The Book of Common Prayer*. This fellowship with worshipers of the past keeps us from feeling that our existence is isolated. As we think of time stretched out behind us and ahead of us, we gain fresh images and concepts of eternity and a new perspective of now. This expands our worship environment at a time when there is much that reduces and confines our worship within our little world.

Hymnals connect the present to the past. Hymns from several centuries in one book have long been accepted by congregations of every Christian tradition. But now the worship planner is called upon to search beyond the hymnal (after a thorough search *of* the hymnal) and beyond their particular tradition for worship material. Fellowship with Christian worshipers from ages past is an important entry point into worship for many young adults who want to find their place in the overarching story or meta-narrative of Christianity.

We can draw great strength from the prayers, songs, and testimonies of worshipers who have gone before us; great strength and hope. The hope is that our good work in the development of worship might stretch into the future, creating fellowship that has come to us, but will not end with us. This kind of fellowship allows us to see how worship has developed over the ages, which is an encouragement to us to make changes in our worship that both speaks to our time and leans forward.

DENOMINATIONAL MIGRATION

The pews of Baptist congregations are not populated by Baptists only. No doubt this is true for every Christian tradition and denomination. People choose their places of worship for a variety of reasons. Denominational affiliation is only one of those reasons. Provisions for children, mission opportunities, music, preaching, and convenient location are also on the list, perhaps even higher on the list.

This phenomenon presents fellowship opportunities and challenges. Liturgical and free-church traditions now share ideas and methods that were unknown or foreign to each other in years past. In the sharing, preaching pedagogy moves from one side to the other, passing lectionaries and church calendars going the other way. Musical styles and advent wreaths are exchanged like Christmas gifts, to the delight of both traditions. Clergy round out their education in seminaries of Christian traditions other than their own. In many locations, weekly ministerial lunches are becoming less denominationally exclusive. This is a good thing, because ministers from the various denominations can share ideas and teach each other the basics of their worship in an informal setting.

As these exchanges become less experimental and more routine, congregations find themselves better fitted to welcome the Christian brothers and sisters once considered Christian cousins because of their tradition of origin. These are acts of Christian unity, hospitality, and fellowship. Again, fellowship serves to teach us, broadening our understanding of our place in the larger Christian scene.

Even with denominational migration, doctrines remain important and distinctive to each host tradition. But, happily, in many cases the doctrines are being reduced from barricade to speed-bump for those who, for one reason or another, are traveling in new directions to participate in worship. To change metaphors from driving to eating, this type of doctrinal fellowship and sharing is not unlike a fellowship or potluck meal in your church. Each person brings a different dish that is enjoyed by everyone. But, at the end of the day, you still have your recipe and your bowl. Much was shared and enjoyed, but nothing was lost. (This analogy breaks down when one considers the number of casserole dishes, bowls, and plates left in the church kitchen, even with names on them. We will not try to draw a parallel there.)

To facilitate all this, the worship planner/leader must learn additional liturgical vocabulary, names, rituals, and symbols. How these new features are introduced is a matter of timing and trust, different, no doubt, for each congregation. An added benefit to all this is seeing our traditions through new eyes, restoring the rich meaning that may have faded because of familiarity over a period of decades, even centuries. This is often true of our worship practices such as baptism and the Lord's Supper.

BAPTISM AND THE LORD'S SUPPER

Baptism underscores fellowship. Getting wet washes away all pretence. You have washed your hands in the public restroom only to discover there are no more towels and there is no blow-dry machine. You must walk back out into the world with hands dripping. It takes a bit of resolve because you are no longer neat and tidy and the world knows where you have been. When you get caught in the rain without an umbrella, you enter the building looking nothing like you had planned to look at that moment. In both cases there is a certain baptism into reality and humility.

In the Baptist tradition, one is purposefully drenched into a new reality in front of God and everyone. In other traditions where pouring or sprinkling is the method, what resembles a child's water prank carries with it the deep significance of eternity itself; humbling. In each case, fellowship is declared and produces warm and understanding smiles. Worship planners, a humble suggestion: when the flow and guidance of the Holy Spirit call for Baptism, do not hide it from worship, or tag it on to worship. Present it as a profound act of worship that surrenders self to God.

The Lord's Supper activates the deep fellowship of eating together. Even the most experienced, even jaded, worshiper senses the deep spiritual significance of participating in the Lord's Supper, no matter the frequency or infrequency of the celebration. If in baptism we stepped into the Jordan, with the Lord's Supper we cautiously step into the upper room to take our place in the fellowship of the original disciples. As significant and declarative as it is, baptism (usually) happens just once, but the table causes us to remember our discipleship on a recurring basis. Every time we eat at this table, we remember that Peter and Judas did, too. We are to eat in remembrance of Jesus, and we do. But we cannot forget those other guys, so we eat in full awareness of our betrayals. As we participate in the Lord's Supper, we are in the fellowship of brothers and sisters, disciples, and sinners. But, we are in the fellowship of sinners saved by grace. This is an entry point into worship for many people. It is fellowship of the richest sort.

Blest be the tie that binds our hearts in Christian love;
The fellowship of kindred minds is like to that above.

Before our Father's throne we pour our ardent prayers;
Our fears, our hopes, our aims are one, our comforts and our
cares.

We share our mutual woes, our mutual burdens bear;
And often for each other flows the sympathizing tear.

When we asunder part, it gives us inward pain;
But we shall still be joined in heart, and hope to meet again.[5]

---

[5] Hymn "Blest Be the Tie That Binds." John Fawcett (1740-1817)

CHAPTER FIVE

Entering Through the Place

> The concept of "place" could receive no higher commendation than this, "I go to prepare a place for you" (John 14:2). Our places of worship, no matter how grand or modest, serve as reminders that Jesus has gone to prepare a place for us. Our places of worship are places of tangible hope. They are a promise big enough and sure enough to walk into and sit down. We must respect our places of worship for this.

The room speaks. It cannot be silenced. The room, in which you worship, gymnasium, abandoned grocery store, or cathedral, speaks. It comments on what is attempted there. The worship planner would do well to work in harmony with the room. The space in which your congregation meets to worship can make something happen or it can shut something down before it ever gets started.

Think of the space that goes unnoticed until garlands are draped across it at the beginning of Advent. Think of the "contemporary" services that have been started in ornate and stately sanctuaries, only to be sent away to the gymnasium if they were to survive. The room speaks. Some people who show up on Sunday enter into worship invited by the room itself.

Even an elementary Biblical study of the temple and the synagogue reveals the significance of the place of worship. The place of worship reveals a theology and a relationship. Stepping into a place of worship is stepping into a particular theology. A place of worship is a tangible statement of doctrine. Within those environments, the place of worship is an invitation to worship and an aid.

The fact that there is a place of worship underscores the importance of gathering.

WHAT THE ROOM WILL ACCEPT

The room will accept anything that understands and contributes to the sense of community of those who gather there. It was the community that shaped the room at some point in history, and now the room returns the favor. Actually, the room simply reports what it was told to say. It reflects what has shaped it, becoming a reliable gauge for the likely success or failure of what might be attempted there. A challenge is issued here to the worship planner. Test new ideas by sitting alone in your congregation's worship space, thinking and praying about the idea. Imagine the reading, or the music, or the action happening. How will it be seen, heard, or received by the one who will sit on Sunday where you sit now? The room will tell you. (Yes, the Holy Spirit will use the room to tell you.)

The room will accept new worship ideas that are conceived in authenticity and introduced in humility. What is actually at work here is the worship planner's love and respect for the people who designed and built this room and who worship here. The worship planner respects the Holy Spirit's work in and through this community, both in times past and in the present.

The room will accept seekers who do not yet understand all of its intricacies, but are in awe of them. In like manner, the room will accept seekers who are surprised and intrigued by its simplicity. Who is this God who is grander than this room? Who is this God who is willing to be born, found, and worshiped in such stark simplicity? Both of these questions are entry points of the matrix and entry points into worship. God is in each place, both places, and beyond. It is affirmation that God can enter any heart.

The room will accept what is temporary and only for a season, if, for those moments, what is offered is offered in the context of eternity. The place of worship is, after all, a place where time meets eternity. But eternity must be present. "Disposable" litanies, songs, readings, and prayers must connect earth's moment and Heaven's eternity, for both are present in the room. A notable proponent of the idea of "disposable" hymns is the Dutch hymn writer and United Reform minister, Fred Kaan (b. 1929). His first hymns, published in *Pilgrim Praise*[6], were written in concert with his sermons with the shared purpose of connecting the specific issues of the day to the truth of the gospel and the hope of eternity. He had no notion of his hymns having a life beyond their particular Sunday. Seeing the important connection of time and eternity led Kaan to write a number of hymns that have proven to be both timely and timeless.[7] If the connection is made, the room will allow the temporary, and worship will happen.

WHAT THE ROOM WILL REJECT

The room will reject non-sense. Here, non-sense means something that might make sense somewhere else, but does not make sense in this space. A common example can be seen in praise teams setting up and attempting to lead worship surrounded by organ pipes and stained glass. The room often speaks more loudly than the praise band, eventually, overcoming it. Yet, in that same environment, folk music might flourish. No "rules" are suggested here, nor is this a commentary on particular styles. The point being made is that any worship style or music style must be in harmony with the room.

A room's sensibilities can be changed. That is called remodeling. Remodeling the worship space is no small undertaking for a congregation. The weight of remodeling is not in its cost, alone. In fact, it could be argued that the financial cost can rise no higher than second place on the list of remodeling concerns. The top concern is "why?"

---

[6] Fred Kaan. *Pilgrim Praise*. (Norfolk, England: Galliard, 1972).

[7] For further discussion of the concept of "disposable" hymns, see: Harold M. Best, *Music Through the Eyes of Faith* (SF: HarperSanFrancisco, 1993), Chapter 1, "God's Creation, Human Creativity, and Music Making," et. al. and Brian Wren, *Praying Twice* (Louisville: Westminster John Knox Press, 2000), Chapter 4, "' Some Demand a Driving Beat,'" et .al.

"Why remodel?" Does remodeling imply that we are changing what we believe about worship? Are we changing what the room will say *to* us and *about* us? Are we "restructuring" our worship? Remodeling a worship center can be done, but it is a big deal.

The room will reject flippant ideas and whims concerning worship. The room stands as a monument (though not static) to the permanence of worship, the foundation that is worship, and our commitment to worship. Those are lifelong (and beyond) principles that will not tolerate fads; trends, maybe; explorations, yes; but passing fancies, no. In a sense, the room is a reminder to ourselves etched in stone, steel, or wood. The room will remember when we do not. That is one of the reasons we build sanctuaries.

WHAT THE ROOM WILL ENHANCE

The room will enhance anything that reveals, or even explores, the deeper purposes of why the room was built. The phrase "why the room was built" is telling. Designing a sanctuary that serves only the purpose of worship in our day is often considered extravagant. More and more worship centers are designed to facilitate worship on Sunday and something else throughout the week. In the first instance, worship is presented as something different and set apart; something special enough to rate its own dedicated space. In the second example, worship is presented in more routine terms; one of the things that goes on here, not necessarily the most important. The worship planners' options are laid out before them, defined for them, in either case. These parameters of worship expanded and set apart as something special or confined and made to conform as something routine, will be sensed by the worshiper as well. This line of thinking is not meant to be judgmental, critical, or limiting. Let it be written clearly and read clearly…some congregations have few or no options at the point of multiple usage space. Such financial considerations, however, should be seen in light of the alabaster jar broken at the feet of

Jesus (Matthew 26: 6-13). The truth is, *all* worship planners must deal with the realities of the room, and, under the guidance of the Holy Spirit, open what doors can be opened into the vastness of Christian worship.

If your worship space is that on Sunday morning, then a dining hall on Sunday evening, and a gymnasium during the week, you have the responsibility and the opportunity to explore the worship implications within the deeper purposes of why the room was designed as it was. The room will enhance that exploration in the context of worship. You may rejoice in the "gymatorium's" versatility, or you may lament its lack of reverence. Either way, the community has spoken and has told the room what to say. Your call is to explore the worship options that can happen there. There may be more of a variety of options than you think. Consult with the Holy Spirit about it.

The flip side of that coin is this: the worship leader whose room is cathedral-esque is not yet in heaven. Specifically dedicated worship space asks the same question. What worship exploration is there to be done here? In both rooms being considered, the worship planner must consider what the worshipers see and sense when they walk into the room for worship. That is your room's door into the matrix of worship, leading into the vast expanse, and, eventually, common experience of Christian worship. The place of worship should not be the warehouse of worship, no matter the intent or restrictions of its architecture. It should be the lobby one passes through to begin a journey into worship.

The room will enhance innovation and creativity that builds upon the liturgical foundation it offers. No matter how one interprets the creation accounts in the book of Genesis, it is obvious that creation is still underway. Hawaii's Big Island is bigger than it was on day one. Pillars of smoke and fire give testimony to that fact. Bigger still, the universe is expanding. We can see it. The Hubble Space Telescope was recently tuned up to do its breathtaking work of standing in earth's position on the expansion timeline, looking backward and forward along the continuum.

It does not seem a stretch to step over into a consideration of the expansive nature of worship as we consider the vastness of God. In our worship, it is beneficial and awe-inspiring to look backward and forward; to explore the wonders of what has happened before our time in the name of worship and to explore the wonders of what lies ahead as we stretch toward heaven and into the mysteries of God in our worship. The room helps us, and not just in looking back. In its own way, and from the unique vantage point it affords, the place of our worship enhances our creative and innovative exploration of worship.

The room speaks. It speaks of us and our understanding of worship, but no matter how loudly it speaks, it cannot overcome the whispering of the Holy Spirit who bids us to explore the mysteries of God through worship.

LEARNING FROM OTHER PLACES

One of the best ways to see and hear your room through fresh eyes and ears is to visit other places of worship. You may not be able to do so on Sunday, but visiting during the week when there is no one in there is beneficial. What does the worship space that is different than yours say to you when you walk in and are the only one there? Take notes. What do you understand about these surroundings? What do you not understand? Do the things you do not understand frustrate you or intrigue you? Remember, worship should leave you with at least as many questions as answers. As you look and think, this unfamiliar room may well be ushering you into worship, with no one else around. If so, what is bringing it about? This encounter with a room that "speaks a different language" refreshes your senses when you think of your worship space back at the church and the visitors who might walk in. But what about the folks who are members there, who worship there every week? Can the room speak to them as vividly? Yes. The specific elements of worship selected by the planner can bring fresh awareness to the long-time member and the new worshiper at the same time, inviting both to enter into worship through the portal of "place." An easy and obvious way to accomplish this might be to have a reading or litany, new to your congregation, lead from an untraditional location in the sanctuary. It's simple. But if the new location illustrates something within the reading, it can be a double encounter for the worshiper; an encounter with the words and with the place.

WHEN THE PLACE IS NOT A ROOM

What if the place of worship is under an interstate highway overpass, as is the case with *Church Under the Bridge* in Waco, Texas? What if the place of worship is an outside location in a retreat setting? In both situations and many others that are similar, worship planning of some sort still must take place, however simple. In settings such as these, the environment still speaks, commenting on God and the worship of God. The vastness of an open night sky ushers us into worship by speaking of the majesty and grandeur of the Creator. The noise and concrete of streets and highways ushers us into worship by speaking of the humility and love of the Savior. These are quite different starting points, but both are true and real. The Holy Spirit speaks, interpreting the particular place's invitation and commentary on worship. Heaven and earth meet in both places.

Another congregation in Waco, Texas, *DaySpring Baptist Church*, gathers around a cattle watering trough when worship is gathered around baptism. With the congregation's new buildings on one side and a hillside gently sloping toward a creek on the other side, the trough is where it was when it was the only structure in a tree-lined pasture. The place is an entry point into worship as reborn Christians are eased into a trough, even as the newborn Christ was eased into a manger. The worship that takes place there is simple. There will be a short, congregational reading from the printed bulletin carried down the hill from the sanctuary, and a simple chorus or hymn carried in the hearts of the community, and the simple, profound beauty of baptism. The reading and the chorus are always in harmony with the place.

GOD DOES NOT LIVE HERE

In chapter two, we considered poetry in the context of the words of worship. Poetry has truth at its surface, but it is truth that points to a deeper truth still. In similar fashion, our place of worship should turn our hearts toward God, but God does not live in the place of our worship. The place of worship, the room, must tell the truth about God at its surface, but it cannot tell it all. No human structure of wood or words can. Neither should the room imply, nor should worshipers assume, that God is defined and confined within the ornate or simple symbolism. The place of worship is an entry point into worship precisely because it functions like poetry. It ushers and encourages those who gather there toward deeper truth, toward the mystery of God.

God cannot be placed in a box, not even one as big as a church, not even one as big as our imagination. No longer is God in the Ark of the Covenant behind the veil. The veil has been torn in two (Matthew 27:51). We got in and God got out, and the place of worship continues to be a place of coming and going. Neither is God in our house of worship. God comes and goes with us *and* meets us there as we gather. Its just one of the mysteries related to God's presence among us and within us. We worship God in the place of corporate worship, but we are not away from God when we leave. The worship leader can make this clear.

God lives where we live. God is in heaven, and God is with us. The place of worship can help us consider the wonder of that truth and its implications. Worship planner/leader, being one of the gatekeepers at this port of entry, is an important responsibility indeed. Each element of worship should, in some way, help the worshiper encounter, again, and perhaps with a bit more understanding, at least a bit more awe, God's omnipresence: here yes, but not just here; with and in me, yes, but not just me; our community, yes, but not just ours; our liturgy, yes, but not just ours. Neither our worship nor our place of worship should presume to have discovered or set God's boundaries. Our worship should explore the boundlessness of God's love and mercy. Worship planner, take note. Work at exploring worship's possibilities. Open yourself to worship's possibilities. This is done through prayer, reading, and Bible study. New ideas will come that can be translated into elements and experiences of worship.

It becomes apparent that worship planning can, indeed, be worship, in and of itself. Equally apparent is the fact that the place of worship is a place that houses starting points rather than ending points.

I GO TO PREPARE A PLACE FOR YOU

The concept of "place" could receive no higher commendation than this, "I go to prepare a place for you" (John 14:2). Our places of worship, no matter how grand or modest, serve as reminders that Jesus has gone to prepare a place for us. Our places of worship are places of tangible hope. They are a promise big enough and sure enough to walk into and sit down. We must respect our places of worship for this. Our worship planning must make use of this fact in every way possible through our words and music and awareness of space.

If place matters for eternity, it must matter here and now. One of the ways in which place matters here and now is that our place of worship is a place of peace. "Do not let your hearts be troubled," this is the beginning of Jesus' discourse on the place he is preparing (John 14: 1 NRSV). Peace and promise are there for us to touch in the places where we meet to worship; Jesus' peace and promise.

The place that Jesus prepares is a dwelling place, a place to "be." We would do well to see the places we prepare, and the worship for which we prepare them, in the context of the heavenly work of Jesus. Think of our worship and our places of worship in the context of "being" rather than "doing" or "accomplishing." This is not a new idea, but like many other important and foundational truths, we must be reminded of them from time to time. Worship as being and the place of worship as refuge from all of the world's pressure toward "doing"; these are heavenly concepts that can contribute in meaningful ways to worship. Indeed, these very thoughts, expressed in the place and plan of worship, can be corridors through which people are ushered into worship.

Preparing the place of worship includes concerning ourselves, as worship planners and leaders, with how the place is adorned. We take great care in how the place of worship is decorated ("adorned" seems a more appropriate word) at Christmas and Easter. Similar care should be taken in the "ordinary" times of worship as well. For the congregations that pay no attention to the ecumenical "church year," displaying the liturgical colors that change from time to time can be an enriching introduction to the significance of adorning the place of worship. For the congregation that adheres to the liturgical calendar, adorning the place of worship faces the challenge of overcoming dulling familiarity. The new color is noticed on the first Sunday of the new season, but quite possibly taken for granted in the weeks that follow. These are positive thoughts, but there are some negative aspects of adorning the place of worship.

Knowing that Jesus is preparing a place for us, our preparation of the place of worship should have the same focus: God's love for us, and in response, our love for God. It is possible for the adorning of our place of worship to slip into decorating it, an issue mentioned a bit earlier. We adorn our place of worship when the things included or added speak of the majesty of God, the love of Christ, and the work of the Holy Spirit. We adorn our place of worship when what we bring in speaks of our devotion to God, our obedience and full submission of heart, mind, and soul, to God.

We simply decorate when we bring into the sanctuary items that distract from our focus on and worship of God. Decorations that divert our attention away from God are at least improper preparations, and may well border on idolatry. The place of worship must be adorned in worshipful ways, not decorated in distracting ways. The "place" as an entry point into authentic worship demands it. I have seen, fashioned in ceramics, an image of Santa Claus bowing before the manger. Thankfully, it was on a shelf in a conference room and not in the place of worship. But the image is stark enough to open our eyes to more subtle misguided decorations. Christmas trees instead of Chrismon trees come to mind. What is the difference? Christmas tree ornaments include secular images as well as religious images. Chrismon trees, by definition, include only symbols of Christ as ornaments. Are these pages heading off on an extreme tangent? I think not. We are discussing the importance of preparing a place that will be an entry point into worship, authentic worship of the One-in-Three.

"Preparing a place" has led some to decorate with flags and others to adorn with banners. "How does the American flag turn our attention to God as supreme, above all and beyond all? How does it turn our hearts toward Jesus, our Lord and the prince of peace? How does it speak of the Holy Spirit as our Comforter and Guide? How does it speak of the hope of Heaven and our primary citizenship?" These words are penned by a former Marine who is the son of a retired Marine.

"I go to prepare a place for you," Jesus said. We take our cue from that and set out to prepare a place for him, not a place for Jesus to live, but a place for Jesus to be worshiped in the context of the Trinity; our God who has made unmistakably clear that we are to have no other Gods (Exodus 20).

We are to have no other Gods in our hearts or represented in the place we prepare for worship. Does the Christian flag represent Jesus, the person, the Christ, or Christianity, the movement, the concept? Worship planner, you must ask these questions. The place must be an entry point into the worship of God, in three persons, with no distractions by anything "that is in heaven above, or that is on the earth beneath, or that is in the water under the earth. [We] shall not bow down to them or worship them; for I the Lord you God am a jealous God..." (Exodus 20:4-5).

And what of banners, are they more adornment than decoration in the context of our working definitions? If banners, like any other element of worship, lead us into the mystery and vastness of God through words and symbols, they adorn the place. If, however, banners reduce our understanding of God or restrict and dictate our response to God, they do not adorn, they merely decorate a place that needs no decoration. The wonder of God is enough. Worship planning must involve open eyes as well as ears and hearts. We must see what the Holy Spirit is saying as well as hear it. What the Holy Spirit shows us is as subtle as what is whispered to us. Both are vital. We must know what we are communicating, and that is not necessarily the same as knowing what we meant to communicate.

Similar questions have been asked concerning crosses, icons, and stained glass windows in the context of Exodus 20. What are the implications of artificial flowers being used instead of real flowers to adorn the worship space? What about art work of any and every sort? Once again, we discover that rules and seeking answers do not help us as much as living the questions with the guidance of the Holy Spirit. As worship planners, we will not always make the best choices. We are human. But we will make fewer poor choices if we will continue to ask, "Why?" "Why are we bringing this item of decoration or adornment into the place of worship?" "What does this item actually say to the worshiper?"

Jesus' work of preparing a place should set us to the work of preparing a place that honors God and opens doors to worship for those who will enter only, or most readily through the invitation(s) the place offers. All doors should be clearly marked.

CHAPTER SIX

Intersecting

Every service is a singular trip through the worship matrix, for each day brings new experience affecting the congregation's mood and thought. New challenges emerge and joys are realized which are to be considered in concert with God's revelation. It is the public walk through the matrix which prompts the worshiper's inner journey.

Come Sunday, people will gather in churches large and small, rich and poor, near and faraway. The congregations will not all look alike, nor will they share a common language. The worship styles will be many, the songs not all the same, and in matters of faith and practice there will be no unanimity.

Every congregation, however, will have a gathering place–indoors, outdoors, hut, or sanctuary–where it will worship. In every place, the service will have a beginning and an end; what happens in between and how it came to be may not even be questioned by the worshipers. If they were to ask, however, they would be told that days, weeks, or even months earlier someone in their faith community prayed, searched, imagined, and prayed some more until the service that was right for the particular Sunday in the particular place became known. Their planner took a journey through scripture, tradition, experience, and memory selecting from word and song what was meaningful both to him and to the congregation.

It does not matter that people are unaware of his pilgrimage or the time it took. He does not terribly mind when someone does not like the choices he made. He knows the plan began long before he took the first step. He recalls people in his life who showed him the pathways that others had pointed out to them. If he could go back to where it all began, he would no doubt arrive at "In the beginning, God..." So, the planner knows he, like those before him, can only point out where the paths lie and trust that other travelers will make the journey.

Every service is a singular trip through the worship matrix, for each day brings new experiences affecting the congregation's mood and thought. New challenges emerge and joys are realized which are to be considered in concert with God's revelation. It is the public walk through the matrix which prompts the worshiper's inner journey. When the path is an interesting one, she will be attracted to other paths of which the larger group is unaware. The service is like a guided tour through beautiful gardens where everyone is free to venture out to explore and then return to the group. Indeed, the well conceived service encourages such departures. On one occasion, she may find her inspiration in a reading and her neighbor in a song. On the next time, the converse may be true.

As the planner prepares for the journey, so must the congregation. Everyone must pack their own bags and study the map of scripture. Riding piggyback on the planner is not permitted! To worship is to walk with the Spirit down the paths He leads.

INTERSECTION: PEOPLE AND THE WORD

This walk, of course, begins with a personal time of prayer and Bible study. As He did for the planner, the Spirit prepares each member of the congregation for the service to come. A retired pastor I know says that when the music minister and the preacher are both listening to the same Spirit they do not need to know what the other will be doing on Sunday. There is truth to this, but the Spirit has no problem working through a good planning session or a phone call! Nonetheless, this quip should also be applied to everyone, for it is not much different than what the apostle Paul told the Corinthians.

> When you come together, each one has a hymn, a lesson, a revelation, a tongue, or an interpretation. Let all things be done for building up. (1 Corinthians 14:26 NRSV)

The choir brings an anthem, a reader a passage of scripture, and the pastor "a word of instruction." These contributions are expected. Congregations should also allow for activities to come from the members' personal walk with God. Testimonies, prayers, requests for prayer, readings from scripture are some examples. Whether scheduled or not, the purpose of every activity is to strengthen the congregation. Through them the people intersect God's Word.

The service planner helps the people understand that the Word comes from them as well as to them by planning activities that encourage everyone's involvement. These may include the following.

Meditations

Place short devotional readings or quotes in the service order which the worshiper can reflect upon as the service unfolds.

Scripture Readings

Rather than only using a solo reader during the service, allow the congregation to read responsively or with a leader.

Readers from Different Age Groups

When solo readers are used, enlist them from all age groups, including children.

Song Lyrics Included in Worship Bulletin

Printing song texts not sung by the congregation helps everyone know the poetic content of the song. Some congregations project the lyrics on large screens, but this method can be a visual distraction and cause the performance to look programmed and insincere. In either case, copyright clearance must be obtained.

Scriptural Allusions

Many songs allude to or directly quote scripture. Print or project the references along with the title information so that the worshipers have the option of reading the associated texts.

Written Responses

Provide space in the worship bulletin for people to write their reflections. Some churches provide such space for sermon notes, but also suggest that notes be taken on the entire service.

Response Wall

Place large sheets of paper in the foyer with markers where the congregation might post their responses to the Word heard in the service. (The wall is not a place to review the sermon.)

Testimony

Ask church members for brief testimonies of what they have learned through the worship experiences at church.

Whenever the Word intersects with people, familiar paths through the matrix are established. The paths of one service join the paths of another, forming a vast roadmap of avenues pleasant to travel.

> Thus says the Lord: Stand at the crossroads, and look, and ask for the ancient paths,where the good way lies; and walk in it, and find rest for your souls.
> (Jeremiah 6:16 NRSV)

INTERSECTION: THE WORD, PEOPLE, AND THE SONG

Words make music. Poetry, even the non-metrical kind, has a certain rhythm, syllables their inflection, and phrases an ebb and flow that the sensitive composer translates into pitch, rhythm and musical line. A good tune complements the text in the way a good marriage enhances each personality. The emotion of the text is conveyed by a tune, subtle nuances highlighted, and something of the nebulous impulse that led to the poem's writing experienced by the singer and the listener.

The best songs transcend time and place. They have an elemental, human quality about them. Songs of varying themes and styles such "Silent Night," "Amazing Grace," or "A Mighty Fortress is Our God" continue to have meaning long after they were first sung. The riches of great songs multiply with time as they intersect with a congregation's heart becoming the testimonies of its faith, tutors of its theology, and the language of its prayer. Songs are the aural expression of the worship matrix the congregation travels.

It is possible, however, to sing a song detached from this depth of meaning and experience. The rhythm of a poem can be exploited, providing a musical groove apart from the truth of the text. Music, rather than intersecting with the Word, can bypass it to revel in its own glory. For example, a severe incongruity occurs when a congregation dances to the beat of a song about Christ's suffering on the cross–"The Old Rugged Cross" set to a swing rhythm.

Singers and arrangers sometimes defend their work saying, "We're giving the songs back to the people." It's true, a new tune set to an older text or a new arrangement of an older tune can illumine a song. Care, though, must be taken that the arrangement does not overshadow the truth of the text while highlighting the personality and skills of the performers. The voice of the congregation is diminished when the singing is surrendered to the trained musicians in a misguided attempt to bring "excellence" to worship. The voice of the congregation is diminished when the songs are arranged as material for the "Christian artist" or "worship leader" with congregational backup. The voice of the congregation is diminished when it is buried by the volume of the drums, the pipe organ, or the guitar.

"Away with the noise of your songs" cried Amos, the prophet. (Amos 5:23 NIV)

Songs are sanctuaries, places of meditation, where worshipers intersect the truth and join voices in chorus with one another. This intersecting of Word, people and song requires careful consideration as to how the song will be sung. Some techniques that can help a congregation intersect with the Word through song include the following.

Change the Tune

New settings of familiar texts reintroduce a congregation to the Word in the songs. The best tunes avoid tricky rhythms or alternating meters that pull the congregation away from contemplating the text to trying to sing it. "The Solid Rock" set to the tune Veni Emmanuel is an example of an effective tune change. The text, "O Come,

O Come Emmanuel," usually associated with this tune will also provide unsung commentary with the new association.

Change the Meter

A meter change provides a new setting while keeping the familiarity of text and tune. Singing the "Coronation" tune of "All Hail the Power of Jesus' Name" to three beats per measure rather than four offers a contemplative mood with the singing of this great text.

Sing A cappella

There is no more beautiful sound than the unaccompanied voices of a congregation. Singing without instruments is a moving and sincere expression of a congregation's voice.

Use a Variety of Instrumental Solos and Accompaniments

The tonal color of various instruments helps worshipers experience a song in new and different ways. Simple instrumental expressions such as a harmonica or an unaccompanied flute can be very effective. You will find a variety of hand bell, piano and organ accompaniments, and orchestrations online in the Worship Matrix.

Hum the Song

Ask the congregation to hum the song as it considers the text. There is an added benefit to this technique as there are, no doubt, people in your congregation who say they cannot sing. Get them accustomed to humming, and one day they may graduate to the choir!

Alternate the Voices

Sing a song with different voice combinations such as a solo on the stanza and the congregation on the refrain; men on one stanza and women on another; children then adults. You get the idea. While one group is singing, the other group is considering the Word. This is often what is happening when individuals are staying silent as the congregation sings.

Let the Congregation Be the Choir

Use all the techniques described above in a congregational anthem. These special arrangements are available online in the Worship Matrix. Your congregation will experience the dynamic of singing in the choir, and the experience just may bring you some choir members.

It is important to introduce new singing techniques slowly. The goal is to help worshipers intersect the Word–not confuse them.

The congregation should learn new songs. God's Word has not been exhausted by the church's musical repertoire nor can it be. Every generation brings fresh material to the church's song heritage. When today's generation learns a song from yesteryear, it receives a gift from the past. When an older generation sings the songs of a new one, it connects to a future it will not live to see. Through songs old and new, eternity is realized–which is why new songbooks are required.

INTERSECTION: THE WORD, PEOPLE, SONG, AND THE PLACE

One quiet Hawaiian evening, I stood outdoors surveying the wreckage around me. The old "termite palace" that had been the church education building was no longer. The demolition was intentional, undertaken to make way for a new building in its place. A few hours earlier, the church members had cheered the destruction, but the quietness and solitude of this moment brought a twinge of sadness. I had not realized how connected this pile of crumbled beams, shattered glass, and broken plaster was to the "life" which had transpired there. Children happily ascended to Sunday School the concrete steps which now led to nowhere. At my feet lay the image of a bird torn from a mural the youth group had painted in the room with the high ceiling which was now an empty hole in the air. The old adage that the church is "not the place but the people" brought little comfort. I knew then what the old-timers mean when they refer to the church building as "God's house."

A place becomes special when Word, people, and song intersect there. Even as pilgrims make their way to Holy land to walk where Jesus walked, all Christians know hallowed places where they have met God. When Jesus said that the true worshipers would "not worship in Jerusalem or this mountain..." he was not negating the importance of place but merely stating that those were not the only spots where God could be found. He knew because he himself met the Father in the wilderness, on the Mount of Olives, and at Gethsemane.

The Word preached, the Word sung, and the Word lived attaches itself to place. To revisit the place is to revisit the Word known there. Like Bethlehem's stable, it need not be a cathedral; the living Word can be found in any old, ordinary place. Even a closet with the door shut, Jesus tells us, can harbor the Lord God Almighty.

Before the turn of the millennium, a friend, Richard Baker, fought a battle with lung cancer. Not given any hope of a cure, he left family, friends, and the congregation he loved to receive alternative treatment in another state. During Holy Week, he wrote the members of the Holy Trinity Episcopal Church in Garland, Texas. Though the battle was eventually lost, Richard's eternal connection to that congregation is beautifully expressed in this excerpt from his letter.

> *I remember a Thanksgiving eve service–the moment of lowering the kneeler as we confessed together our sins–and suddenly becoming aware that there was one particular spot along that kneeler which was somehow more comfortable than the others. Of course, I'd always known this was true on one level–all of us instinctively move to those small indentions when we're kneeling. But somehow that night, it struck me just exactly why it felt so much better to kneel there. It was because so many other people had knelt there before me. And on that night as on this, I felt so blest to be a part of that heritage of faith and devotion–of the Holy Trinity Saints both here and there, both now and then–that have paved the way for me with their steadfast commitment to our Lord.*

The psalmist said, "I love the place where your glory dwells..." The glory of "God with us" becomes associated with walls, floors, ceiling, space, and light.

Every place has its strengths. A stage lighting system is hung in one room while beautiful light pours through the stained-glass windows of another. A cathedral with vaulted ceilings turns thoughts to heaven while another room provides an intimacy not possible in a cathedral. The worship planner gets acquainted with the room and determines the possibilities. Before he can truly know the room, however, he must see it through the eyes of the people who worship there. First Baptist Waco's worship space is a cruciform structure in the Byzantine style. The room shelters a large pipe organ, and beautiful stained glass including an amazing dome overhead. Entering the room for the first time, one could easily associate it with a formal worship style. However, the building was completed in 1905 at a time when ornate design was fashionable in public gathering places such as theaters, opera houses and later, movie palaces. They were grand places where communities gathered for social events. First Baptist Waco is a gathering place for the Waco community, and though meaningful worship experiences occur there, people do not enter the room in hushed silence but in the joy of being together. Understanding how people view the room guides the planning of the worship that will occur there.

An old house of worship is a gift from earlier generations. Time passes, people come and go, and changes to the space must inevitably be made, but the changes should reflect continuity with what came before. The room for many of the members will have become the visual representation of the inner worship matrix they travel. It calls them to consider word and song. This is the same dynamic at work when familiar music prompts us to worship. New songs may be added to the existing songs, and the worshipers' bearings in the matrix maintained. Over time, the newer songs become so associated with the matrix journey that they too become prompts, and it is less of a problem to drop an old one. So too, a balance should be sought between reconstruction and restoration. Restore the witness of the past while building a new one for the future.

The planner prepares a place on earth for worship as Christ does in heaven, or maybe the planner is only the caretaker of a place Christ has already prepared on earth for worship. Either way, the kneelers are lowered in anticipation of an intersection between Word, people, and song.

THE CONGREGATION INTERSECTS THE WORD, SONG, PEOPLE, AND PLACE

Every person's experience while walking through the matrix is unique. For some walkers, the spoken word makes the greatest impression and for others the word sung. Some delight in the place of worship and others fellowship with the people. These differences are revealed in conversations about the service. A prayer which one person says was a blessing is not remembered by another. A song one thought poorly chosen, another found very moving. This is not a problem, for God did not make everyone the same.

> The gifts he gave were that some would be apostles, some prophets, some evangelists, some pastors and teachers, to equip the saints for the work of ministry, for building up the body of Christ, until all of us come to the unity of the faith and of the knowledge of the Son of God, to maturity, to the measure of the full stature of Christ. (Ephesians 4:11-13 NRSV)

The worshipers receive from and give to the service according to their gifts. "Everyone has a hymn, or a word of instruction, a revelation, a tongue or an interpretation." The goal is for everyone to grow to whatever fullness is intended for them. The service planner knows and accepts that not all activities will be equally engaged. He is not upset that someone is not singing or appears to be daydreaming during the readings. He prays that God will be found wherever that person is in the matrix.

The congregation as a whole also experiences Word, song, people, and place in a unique way which shapes its personality and attracts new members to it. Variations between congregations may appear like this.

Congregation A
word, people, song, place

Congregation B
people, word, song, place

Congregation C
place, song, people, word

Examine church websites and you will note the differences. "We believe the Bible to be God's inspired Word...," begins the description of a word-first church. "Connecting people" reflects a people-first approach of another church family. "You'll find our church to be a place of refreshment in today's complicated world," is the place-first invitation from a third.

How would you arrange the words to describe your congregation? How would the old-timers in the church arrange them? How would the young adults? One order is no more holy than another. There should be no guilt in putting people last and the place first unless people are simply left off the list. Like sunbeams passing through a turning prism, the light shining from word, people, place, and song displays its colorful patterns in many ways.

TRANSFIGURATION

> "Come, let us go up to the mountain of the Lord, to the house of the God of Jacob; that he may teach us his ways and that we may walk in his paths." (Isaiah 2:3 NIV)

The intersecting of word, song, people and place can be found throughout the Biblical narrative. In the Old Testament, the glory of God so filled the temple when the singers sang and the trumpets played that the priests could not minister–an intersection of place and song (2 Chronicles 5:13-14). In the New Testament, 3000 souls were saved on the day of Pentecost following Peter's sermon–an intersection of word and people. Perhaps the most remarkable instance occurred when Jesus took Peter, James, and John on a journey up a mountain.

> And he was transfigured before them, and his face shone like the sun, and his clothes became dazzling white. Suddenly there appeared to them Moses and Elijah, talking with him. Then Pe-

ter said to Jesus, 'Lord, it is good for us to be here..."(Matthew 17:2-4 NRSV)

Jesus, Moses and Elijah had a conversation. Scripture does not detail what was said–only that it took place. This fact alone though is significant, for it represents the intersection of the Old Testament with the New, the Great High Priest with the lawgiver and the prophet. Dramatic yes, but what is just as amazing is that in any ordinary service, the conversation continues and everyone, as disciples, can listen. It can be heard in the reading of scripture, the singing of songs, the preaching of the sermon. The service leader invites today's disciples to travel to where Jesus, Moses, and Elijah are joined by Peter, James, and John and a great host of poets, hymn writers, departed loved ones, and other witnesses celebrating grace.

Yes, every service *can* be a mountaintop experience even without bright lights and transfigured forms. You and I are invited on a journey through the matrix where word and song intersect with people and place. Once we dare to travel, we can only say, like Peter on the mountain, "Lord, it is good for us to be here..."

CHAPTER SEVEN

Entering Through Music Ministry

Whatever their title might be, the person who leads a congregation in worship must purposefully set about the task of getting to know the people. Those who come to worship will be more readily led into worship by someone they know. This does not mean that the minister must be in the homes or work places of every member of a large congregation; not even at every hospital bedside. It does mean that enough of that kind of interaction must take place to establish a reputation of involvement and concern. The ministry must be authentic, of course.

The person who plans and leads worship must not think that their responsibility exists only in the arenas of art and leadership. This person is, or should be, a minister of the first order in their understanding of worship and their relationship to the congregation. They should be deeply aware of a call to usher people into the relationship with God that is called "worship."

How the congregation views the work and ministry of the one who leads them in worship may well be an insight into how they view worship, itself. It is an indicator of what they expect from this person and what they expect to happen or to experience in worship.

The one who leads in worship is a gatekeeper; a gatekeeper and for some, the gate, itself, when it comes to entering into worship.

A ROSE BY ANY OTHER NAME

In his well-known and oft quoted play *Romeo and Juliet*, Shakespeare asks a question of humankind that echoes to this day in venues as diverse as flower shop slogans and university philosophy courses. "What's in a name?" he asks, "That which we call a rose by any other word would smell as sweet."(II, ii, 1-2) A rose may be a rose, but a minister/musician "by any other word" may be a different kind of flower.

We have watched this particular rosebud over the past several decades as it has blossomed in the "free-church" tradition. Observations, from earliest to most recent, include these titles: *Song Leader, Minister of Music, Associate Pastor (Music), Minister of Music and Worship, Worship Pastor, Worship Leader, Lead Worshiper, Worship Producer, Celebration Pastor,* and *Minister of Magnification.* Something is going on. It is a long road between *Song Leader* and *Minister of Magnification.* One imagines an intriguing journey. One title that has remained unchanged throughout the full length of the journey is *Organist/Choirmaster.* This title can be found in both free-church and liturgical traditions. It has not changed. Its wording, too, is succinct and purposeful. It tells its story.

The fact that the list is as long as it is indicates that one title does not fit all situations. Congregations are sending a message to someone as they choose or coin a title for the position. They are declaring a particular theology of worship. The title, then, becomes a significant indicator of how and why that congregation proposes to go forward in the practice of corporate worship. It could be that the congregation's personnel committee is establishing boundaries for the person with the title. Perhaps the title is nothing more than a job description in a nutshell. But the ministry of this person as one of the entry ways into the worship matrix must not be ignored in the selection of a title.

What we do know is that there is never a time that words do not matter in worship. Words always matter in worship: the words of our songs, our prayers, our sermons, and the preferred translation of scripture, the words of institution before the Lord's Supper, and the words that introduce and explain baptism. We have considered these issues in earlier chapters; so, too, the titles (words) given to those who plan and lead our worship; they matter. Let us begin the journey.

TITLES ARE REVEALING

Song Leader has an honest matter-of-factness to it. This congregation expects to sing on Sunday, and they need someone to get them started and stopped. They need someone to hold them together and to carry the tune. Here, worship is more than music. In fact, worship may be other than music. *Worship* and *preaching* may be synonymous here. This title is often found in settings where the person chosen for this position has little or no formal music training. However, they are often recognized as the best musician in the church (other than the pianist). This person must be a member of the congregation, for only a member of the congregation would know their songs and tempos, and how music functions in their midst.

Creativity here is welcomed, but must be, as in any situation, well within the context of the community's experience and giftedness. Any tendency toward change or creativity in the context of worship planning or worship leadership will be approached cautiously. You could bring in a donkey for the Christmas program or an "outside" soloist who is related to a church member in good standing, but probably not a string quartet from the nearest symphony orchestra. This is not a derogatory generality. The people of this congregation have experienced grandeur in nature and seen extravagant stage productions. Neither am I implying ignorance of what worship is, but there does exist a certain satisfaction with their "order of worship" and music's role within that order, and what is authentic expression in the context of their community. The "order of worship" is often as set in its structure as is any "liturgical" form.

If *Song Leader* is the title, and ministry (formal or informal) is evident in the person's relationship to the congregation, the title should be changed. It is part of the larger environment in which worship is planned, led, and understood.

Further, *Song Leader* does not imply either the presence or absence of a choir. The use of this title makes it possible for another person of some musical skill to hold the title of "choir director," if there is a choir. The title *Song Leader* is about helping those who will enter into worship through the singing of their songs. It does not imply any formal assignment or expectations of extended ministry within the congregation. The *Song Leader* may well show up at hospitals and in the homes of those needing help, but this person will show up as a member of the worshiping community, not because of any formal ministerial responsibility. This is a respected and elected position.

Minister of Music appeared on the scene shortly after the end of World War II as returning war veterans and seminaries met in the shade of the G.I Bill of Rights, a federal education funding program. It is a common title even to this day. It implies a pastoral ministry expectation of wide scope and spiritual depth. The apex of the *Minister of Music's* corporate responsibilities was/is the adult choir and detailed planning and preparation of Sunday's worship, excluding the sermon itself. Large, musically agile choirs are often the primary goal of congregations who use the title *Minister of Music*. "Age-graded" choirs involving children three years old through high school are not only seen as ministries to those children and their families, they also serve as "feeder" choirs for the adult choir of their congregation, or of another, similar congregation, when those children grow up and leave home. The minister of music is ultimately responsible for all those choirs and will probably direct one or more of them. Now, senior adult choirs are quite prominent. Again, they are the responsibility of the *Minister of Music*.

The title *Minister of Music* also implies the responsibility and expectation of pastoral ministry to the entire congregation, not just choir members. It is this extra-musical ministerial connection that brings a pastoral element to the *Minister of Music's* worship planning and leading. The *Minister of Music* is perceived by the congregation to be a minister throughout the week, adding credence to his or her worship planning and leadership on Sunday. Toward that end, ministers of music are often ordained into the gospel ministry. They are expected to be able to analyze the theological verity of music selected for use in the life and work of the congregation. The person holding the title and responsibility of *Minister of Music* must be fully reliable and qualified as both minister *and* musician.

When this title is used, the congregation sees worship and ministry and community as braided, intertwined into a whole.

Associate Pastor (Music) is simply an underscoring of the *ministerial* expectations and confidence a congregation has for its *Minister of Music.* This title is often initiated by the pastor as a "step up," for the person and position in question, from *Minister of Music.* Indeed, this person may well be addressed as "*Pastor* Tom," etc. with this title. The actual responsibilities may not change at all as the title moves from *Minister of Music* to *Associate Pastor.* Worship will not be affected by this change. However, the minister's comfort level with his or her role may be affected if the change in title is meant to suggest that more ministerial contact with the congregation is being strongly suggested.

Minister of Music and Worship is similar in intent to *Associate Pastor (Music)* in that it is an underscoring of a portion of the *Minister of Music's* role and relationship within the congregation. In this case, however, it is an underscoring of the place of worship in the person's job description. It is an indication that worship is receiving new focus and, perhaps, elevation in the congregation's consciousness. This renewed focus might stem from a deeper understanding of worship, or, it might stem from a new commitment to church growth, seeing worship as the best way to be perceived as relevant to the surrounding culture. The intent is crucial. It affects the minister's "to-do list" each day and it also affects worship. The intent of adding "*and Worship*" may even challenge how the minister interprets his or her ministerial call, especially if the intent of the change is to turn worship more toward the "un-churched."

Worship Pastor is an intriguing title because ministry once spread across the life and breadth of the congregation seems to be confined, now, to the hour and event designated "worship." The arena for this person's ministry and pastoring is clearly delineated; it is to be in the context of worship. Even so, in many cases, this person is expected to function as a *Minister of Music*. When that is true, the use of the title *Worship Pastor* is simply an announcement that the congregation is aware that worship has become the face of the church and is the "currency" of advertising out in the larger community. Yet, words matter, and the expectations of the congregation for the *Minister of Music* or *Associate Pastor (Music)* have changed a bit. If this person's hospital visits are largely confined to visiting the church's musicians, or if they do not preside at weddings or funerals, it is acceptable. They are the *Worship Pastor*. Certainly, authentic worship is transforming and healing. But a throughout-the-week connection with the congregation is not necessarily implied in the title *Worship Pastor*.

Worship Leader is another common title. This one seems to have the same simple honesty as we saw in the title, *Song Leader*. The expectation seems to be that this person's relationship to the congregation is ministerial only to the extent that worship is a ministry to the congregation. This person, according to the title, is not a pastor, nor does the congregation expect them to be. Ministry by this person beyond Sunday morning's worship might be welcomed, or it might be seen as presuming on the pastor, whose title *does* indicate an on-going ministerial connection to the congregation. One must ask, "If there is no pastoral connection to the congregation, how is this person supposed to know the cares and concerns that accompanied the congregation to this place at this hour?" Will this person be seen by the congregation only on Sunday mornings? Does the congregation expect to see the worship leader only on Sunday mornings? How does that affect the worship planned, led, and experienced? These are not questions about the person's integrity or commitment to God, nor even of their understanding of worship. The questions focus on the congregation's understanding of worship and its connection to everyday life. This person may well know the cares and concerns of the congregation as a member of that community, but will they be afforded a ministerial connection to the congregation that will allow him or her to give spiritual guidance beyond introductions to the next song?

Does the title *Worship Leader* indicate that worship is an hour that can be planned and led by someone who is distanced from the congregation but who qualifies for the position on the basis of being a good musician and sufficiently "spiritual"? Words matter. This person may well be a spiritual leader within the congregation, fully capable of enabling authentic and informed worship, but the title leaves many blanks to be filled in regarding their understanding of worship's place in the full life and work of the congregation. Just because it is subtle, does not mean it is of no consequence. This leads us to the next title; a small change, but one worth noting.

Lead Worshiper symbolically connects the one up front to the congregation. This makes that person a fellow worshiper, but does the title unintentionally suggest "most important worshiper"?

Worship Producer. Worship is, in fact, a drama. But is it to be a production? Let us consider it for a moment. When we enter into worship (note that I did not say, "Enter into the presence of God," a presence we cannot escape) we acknowledge the eternal now of the entire story of God's redemptive work. Christ *is* born today in the now of the eternal day. Christ the Lord *is* risen today. We enter into the ever now, ever unfolding drama of *The Story* when we enter into worship. That is drama of the highest sort.

The congregation that chooses this title for the one up front, at some level, sees their worship as a presentation to be professionally and excellently...produced. This understanding of worship sees the production as the best gift possible to be given to God, and at the same time, something that can gain the attention and, perhaps, the admiration of a TV-movie-savvy society. What does this congregation expect of the person with this title? What does this congregation understand worship to be? Where is the focus of this title? Is there not at least a slight possibility that this title indicates the person's first responsibility is to the technology, equipment, and this week's script? Is this different than the traditional *Minister of Music's* responsibility of proper house lighting, microphones that work, proper rehearsal of the choir, and worship planning?

In this instance, are the gathered people the congregation, the studio audience, or the viewing audience? What *is* the congregation's role in worship? What is the person in the congregation being invited into? These questions are insights into the congregation's understanding of worship.

Our two remaining titles for the person up front will voice some specific ideas about the answer to the question.

Celebration Pastor enunciates a particular viewpoint concerning worship. One wonders if lament or prayers of confession have a place in the hour of worship. It may well be that lament and confession do, indeed, have place here, but what does the title indicate to the one who must enter worship through these portals? Worshipers are human beings, and humans need to worship in environments that acknowledge and embrace the whole truth about life.

Worship can always be a time of thanksgiving (definition of "Eucharist"), even if we are experiencing the joy/anger dichotomy of thankfulness for the strength to make it through a situation that causes us to be angry with God. On the cross, Jesus cried the portion of Psalm 22 that asks, "My God, my God, why have you forsaken me?" That cry can be prayed, even sung as an honest expression of the majesty of God.

Celebration Pastors can weep with us in worship when that is our honest expression, but they may have to step over or around their title to do it. Why give them such an obstacle? Do we want to communicate to the world that life is one big celebration for Christians? Is worship confined to expressions of celebration only? No one would say that it is. I am not suggesting that is the experience or motivation of those who choose this title for the person up front, but we must ask how it affects the leader's ability to usher some into worship.

Minister of Magnification, like *Celebration Pastor,* returns a sense of involvement with the congregation beyond starting and stopping worship, but we are still confined to the worship center. *Minister of Magnification* certainly places the focus back on God and that is good. But the lament question resurfaces, as it must in times of war and hurricane and disease and famine.

Worship cannot be a time of escape from reality. It must be a time of confessing our reality and allowing our reality to be transformed, as prayer and praise works its way up through the pain and pressures of our heart. *Minister of Magnification* does speak of the first and final, overarching, intent of all the elements of worship, separately and as a whole. But happy worshipers will feel more at home, it seems, in this place than will those who are present, honestly, and only, because they remember that this is the right place and right time.

Worship Enlivener is one of the more recent attempts to describe the minister's role. This title conveys a sincere and careful desire to awaken and enrich. One cannot avoid the immediate response, however, of "isn't enlivening worship the work of the Holy Spirit?" The answer might be, "Yes, and the Holy Spirit works through this leader to do that work." The conversation reveals practical theology at work. It is evidence of a mystery explored. Our words fall short when we try to define worship. No wonder then that our titles stretch to describe the work of the brother or sister who leads the weekly, corporate exploration.

Each of these titles speaks to a particular understanding of worship. Each falls short of the worship that is due the one true God, the triune Father, Son, and Holy Spirit. Each of these titles reveals a particular understanding of the relationship between worship, ministry, and community. It is not enough for any of us to be satisfied with our understanding of worship, ceasing therefore to search the scriptures for deeper understanding and purer expression. Such satisfaction would be self-centered and self-serving, demanding nothing, or nothing more, of us in worship. We are to journey through the questions, living them as we go.

MINISTRY CAN OVERCOME

A ministry title that is not what the congregation actually intends can and should be changed. It is a facet of the overall project of worship planning. But an unfortunate title for the leader can be overcome by that person's understanding of worship and ministry and their love for the congregation.

Whatever their title might be, the person who leads a congregation in worship must purposefully set about the task of getting to know the people. Those who come to worship will be more readily led into worship by someone they know. This does not mean that the minister must be in the homes or work places of every member of a large congregation; not even at every hospital bedside. It does mean that enough of that kind of interaction must take place to establish a reputation of involvement and concern. The ministry must be authentic, of course.

Ministry of this sort is essential to attaining the deepest level of worship planning and worship leadership. It is humbling to think that one person could be another person's point of entry into worship. Humble ministry throughout the week will help that level of informed planning and relational leadership become a reality.

The issue of titles need not be an issue of ordination. This is not even an issue of respect for the person. The issue of titles has to do with the congregation's understanding and expectations of worship. It is the proper labeling of this particular worship matrix entry point that is the focus of the conversation.

COOPERATIVE PLANNING

Pastors and those who lead worship's music benefit when they work together to plan worship. More than that, they smooth the path for the congregation to enter into worship. This team effort should not be neglected because of the time worship planning requires.

Nothing the pastor does is more important than participating in worship planning and leadership. The pastor's involvement and interest will be readily detected by the congregation. They will attribute added importance to worship when it is obvious that it matters enough for the pastor to give it time.

Shepherding toward worship by example is an important facet of the pastor's call. The sheep hear the Shepherd's voice. Does the under-shepherd hear it as well? The congregation needs to know that he or she does.

The Other Matrix

Since you have reached the end of this book, it can be assumed that you are in some way responsible for or interested in worship planning. Your title may be that of *Pastor, Song Leader, Minister of Music* or *Minister of Magnification.* You may use the lectionary, build song sets, or simply select the music while driving to church on Sunday morning. Whatever your position or method, it is the authors' hope that within these pages you have realized there is a matrix filled with people on earth and in heaven who, through word and song, rejoice in God's grace.

The worship matrix is open on Sunday morning, and it is open throughout the week. It is open to all who would enter and explore its treasures, fulfilling the deepest desire for authentic worship. Sadly, however, many people never do.

There is another matrix. It is the matrix of business, politics, technology, and entertainment. It is the matrix of buying and selling, of succeeding and failing. In its confines, people are judged by the words they speak, the songs they sing, and the places where they live. Everyone walks its paths including the service planner. He must consider what will be successful at his church and what will not. He considers the kind of music various constituencies find appealing and what activities they find meaningful. He considers what can be done to boost attendance and compares his church stats with those of other congregations. So, living in the "other matrix" must be accepted as a condition of being human.

It is possible, however, to be a resident of both realms, bringing the lessons learned in one to the other. Isaiah said, "Come, let us go up to the mountain of the LORD, to the house of the God of Jacob. He will teach us his ways, so that we may walk in his paths." (Isaiah 2:3, NIV). In one realm we learn God's ways, that we might walk his paths in another. In the worship matrix, the voices heard in word and song, from people and place, help us navigate the maze of the other matrix. And the opportunities and dilemmas we find there drive us to places of refreshment and nourishment in the worship matrix. The service planner knows this and plans experiences that connect things of heaven and things of earth. He knows the congregation will come to church yearning for both revelation and restoration.

If, on some occasions, inspiration seems fleeting and ideas hard to come by, the planner may be encouraged by Paul's letter to the Roman church.

"The word is near you, on your lips and in your heart" (Romans 10:8 NRSV)

The word bubbles up. It is the stream of living water Christ spoke about. The planner, musician or preacher, works and prays knowing that the source will be found. She learns the paths that lead to the wilderness and the paths that lead to refreshment.

There are resources that can help the planner find those paths. One such resource is a website called, like this book, "Worship Matrix"[8], in which you can explore the numerous connections among scripture, hymn texts, meditations, and other readings. As a user, you will discover how prophets, poets, composers, and theologians of diverse cultures and times bore witness to God's truth. The site will point out paths you might not otherwise travel and offer resources to enhance the service at your church. As excellent as it is, however, it alone cannot be your inspiration. Inspiration cannot be downloaded.

---

[8] www.worshipmatrix.com

It does not come in the canvas bag handed out at a worship conference, nor is it found in a single book. It comes from walking the paths of the worship matrix and applying the lessons learned to the other matrix. It comes from voices of the past called forth by a song lyric, a scripture reading, or a choral anthem to speak again. What was spoken long ago prepared you for this moment; now you plan for a moment yet to be.

Inspiration for service leadership comes from surrounding yourself with voices engaged in eternal conversation. It comes as you listen to songs, read books, hear sermons, and visit with friends. It comes as you sit alone in the sanctuary, peruse the hymnal, and study the stained glass.

Inspiration may seem to come in random ways. A Sunday School lesson from childhood links with a contemporary song, which then joins a quote from an early church father. So, too, the activities of a worship service present themselves in many ways to the membership. The service should be not be evaluated only in terms of how point A connects to point B, but how A connects to D and D to B. The service is unified not by its sequence but by the interrelatedness of its elements.

Some years ago while wandering the grounds of the National Cathedral in Washington, D.C., I happened upon something I had not seen before. A large maze-like circular pathway was laid out on the lawn, and people were slowly walking its circuits to a point at its center. A sign at the entrance told me I was looking at a prayer labyrinth. It all seemed somewhat "new age" to me; but intrigued by the faces of the people walking it, I dared to try it for myself and immediately felt its impact. Outside the circle, people lounged on the grass enjoying the late Sunday afternoon as their children ran and played. Inside the circle was another dimension–something that could only be described as holy. Strangers at different points in the circuit slowly passed each other, moving in different directions but toward the same destination. I felt a certain kinship with them, for we were sharing a journey. We were at different places, yet in the same place, silently offering our words and songs to God.

Having reached my destination at the labyrinth's center, I reflected on my walk and what it meant to have arrived. Life is this type of journey, I thought. Even though we walk in circles, there is a center where fellowship with God is found. That is why people keep coming to worship. They are looking for that spot and are willing to travel to get there. Worship planning shows them a path to take.

Rejoicing in my accomplishment, I then realized I had made only half the trip. There was a walk with no shortcuts back to the entrance. The return journey would require the same prayer and determination which brought me to the resting place. Even so in the service, a congregation enters a matrix with a path leading to the center. The center is fellowship with God, and the congregation walks in hope of entering his rest (Hebrews 4). Worship planning lays the path out on the lawn and invites the passersby to enter. But there is also a return path to the edge, where the matrix of worship joins the matrix of daily existence. This walk, like Peter reluctantly leaving the mountain of the transfiguration, is the most important; for by it the transforming power of the worship matrix is carried into the realm of the other matrix. This is the walk we must complete until the "matrix" of this world becomes the "matrix" of our Lord and of His Christ, and He reigns forever. (Revelation 11:15).